Field Guide to the
Grasses, Sedges and Rushes
of the United States

Field Guide to the Grasses, Sedges and Rushes of the United States

EDWARD KNOBEL

REVISED BY
MILDRED E. FAUST
Associate Professor of Botany, Emeritus
Syracuse University

SECOND REVISED EDITION

DOVER PUBLICATIONS, INC.
NEW YORK

Published in Canada by General Publishing Com-
pany, Ltd., 30 Lesmill Road, Don Mills, Toronto,
Ontario.
Published in the United Kingdom by Constable
and Company, Ltd., 10 Orange Street, London
WC2H 7EG.

This Dover edition, first published in 1977, is a
revised edition of the work first published by Bradlee
Whidden, Boston, in 1899 under the title *The
Grasses, Sedges and Rushes of the Northern United
States*. For this edition the scientific and common
nomenclature has been brought up to date, and a
new preface and index prepared, by Mildred E.
Faust.

International Standard Book Number:
0-486-23505-X
Library of Congress Catalog Card Number:
77-72531

Manufactured in the United States of America
Dover Publications, Inc.
180 Varick Street
New York, N.Y. 10014

PREFACE TO THE REVISED EDITION

For this revision the current scientific names are listed by genus and species, with the specific name decapitalized according to the International Code of Botanical Nomenclature, which insures uniformity and a single authentic scientific name for each plant. Common names are not under any code, often being local. Some plants have several common names and a single one may apply to different plants. Although the names have been updated, the order and structure of Knobel's 1899 edition have been retained. One new feature, an index to all genera and common names, has been added.

References used for most of the current names are: A. S. Hitchcock, *Manual of Grasses of the United States* (Dover reprint, 1971); Stanley J. Smith, *Checklist of Grasses of New York State;* K. K. Mackenzie, *North American Cariceae;* Asa Gray, *Manual of Botany,* 8th edition; and H. A. Gleason and A. Cronquist, *Manual of Vascular Plants.* Acknowledgment is given to Stanley J. Smith for his valuable assistance.

MILDRED E. FAUST

INTRODUCTORY

Man's existence depends directly or indirectly, almost entirely on the grasses, a fact which should make this part of the vegetable kingdom the most interesting to us. Aside from their usefulness, their beauty and graceful forms are unsurpassed by any other plants; and, except a few cultivated kinds, they are generally little known because the smallness of their flowering parts on which the student depends to identify them, makes it difficult and tedious to find their names.

A farmer or an experienced agrostologist readily recognizes most grasses by their general appearance, and only in doubtful cases refers to the details. Text books use just the opposite method, leading from the small details to the whole. The system here followed leads gradually from the simplest form of an ear to the most complicated forms, and the student will find this reversed method much easier and simpler. Where grasses have a similar appearance the drawing of the spikelet before each name will insure the student finding the right one. Technical expressions have been avoided as much as possible to make this handbook easier for amateurs. To avoid misunderstandings an explanation of expressions used is here given.

By ear is meant the whole flowering part of a single stem or culm, however complicated and branched. An ear is composed of many small earlets or spikelets, and a spikelet consists of two outer scales, husks or glumes, answering to the calyx of a flower, and containing one, two, or many flowering scales, which enclose the stamens, pistils and fruit; sometimes some flowering scales contain fertile, others sterile flowers.

Spikelets normally one or two-flowered, rarely contain more flowers, but many-flowered spikelets often vary in the number of their flowers. Spikelets on different grass-plants of the same kind differ little in size.

In comparing spikelets observe if their outer scales are of the same length, or one shorter than the other, if pointed or blunt, rough on midrib or not, smaller or larger than the flowering scales, also if the spikelet contains bristles or silky hair inside, and how long these are, compared with the scales.

The heights given are those of medium sizes, and may differ a half one way or the other; for a grass on a barren spot may reach a height of only a few inches, when another of the same kind, on fertile ground, may grow to three or four feet.

The ear to be observed should be fully developed, just after flowering. Many ears undergo considerable changes in their development; they may appear solid or bushy at first, spread to the utmost in flowering time, and contract, droop or collapse when loaded with seed.

As the true grasses are commonly confounded with the wild grasses, sedges and rushes, those included have also been described, somewhat more briefly. They are often interesting on account of the singular shape of their fruit, but are almost useless for foods to man and beast.

The drawings on the plates of Grasses are almost life-size, though for the larger kinds a small ear has been represented.

The spikelets are twice natural size, except those of the brome grasses, which are life size.

For the Sedges and Rushes the plates are about two-thirds life size, and in these instead of spikelets, the fruit pouch and its bract or supporting leaflet has been represented twice their natural size.

GENERAL KEY

Seed single in each flowering scale.

Stem hollow, with few exceptions, round or flattened, jointed.

Sheath of leaves open at the back.

TRUE GRASSES. *Gramineæ.*

Stem solid, mostly triangular or round, not jointed.

Sheath of leaves closed at the back.

WILD GRASSES. SEDGES. *Cyperaceæ.*

Seeds several in each pouch.

Stem solid, mostly round, flowers regular, consisting of three outer and three inner scales, and one pouch containing the seeds.

RUSHES. *Juncaceæ.*

KEY TO THE GRASSES. *Gramineæ.*

5

1. TIMOTHY. *Phleum pratense* L. 2½ ft. high; ear 3½ in. long, ear upright and stiff, no bristles, but sharp awns on the glumes. Much cultivated, found everywhere in fields, meadows and roadsides.

2. MEADOW FOXTAIL. *Alopecurus pratensis* L. 1½ ft. high; ear 2 in. long, uppermost leaf shorter than its sheath, bristle short. In meadows.

3. MARSH FOXTAIL. *Alopecurus geniculatus* L. 1 ft. high; ear 2 in. long, bristle as long as spikelet, upper leaf as long or longer than its sheath; otherwise like No. 2. In marshes.

4. GREEN FOXTAIL or BRISTLEGRASS. *Setaria viridis* (L.) Beauv. 2 ft. high; ear 3 in. long, green, ear flexible, sometimes interrupted at the lower end; bristles upward barbed, longer than the spikelet. In fields.

5. FOXTAIL MILLET. *Setaria italica* (L.) Beauv. 4 ft. high; ear 8 in. long, yellowish or purplish, thick, nodding; often interrupted in branch-like clusters at the lower end; bristles upward barbed. Much cultivated in fields.

6. YELLOW FOXTAIL or BRISTLEGRASS. *Setaria lutescens* Hubb. 3 ft. high; ear 3 in. long, tawny yellow, bristles upward barbed. In fields.

7. BUR BRISTLEGRASS. *Setaria verticillata* (L.) Beauv. 1½ ft. high; ear 2½ in. long, pale green, bristles downward barbed. About dwellings.

8. SWEET VERNALGRASS. *Anthoxanthum odoratum* L. 1½ ft. high; ear 1¾ in. long, sometimes interrupted at its lower end. Sweet scented when drying. The earliest grass in spring. Everywhere.

9. AMERICAN BEACHGRASS. *Ammophila breviligulata* Fern. 3 ft. high; ear 12 in. long, whitish, thick; leaves very long and narrow. (The drawing is half size.) On sandy sea shores.

10. ALPINE TIMOTHY. *Phleum alpinum* L. 1 ft. high; ear 1 in. long. Similar to crippled Timothy grass No. 1. On high mountains.

11. CANARYGRASS. *Phalaris canariensis* L. 2 ft. high; ear 1 in. long. The seed is the common food for canary birds. About dwellings.

12. RABBITFOOT GRASS. *Polypogon monspeliensis* (L.) Desf. 1½ ft. high; ear 2½ in. long. From Europe or Asia. Near the coast.

See also REED CANARYGRASS, pl. VI; *Spartina*, pl. VIII.

PLATE I

1. RYE. *Secale cereale* L. 5 ft. high; ear 5 in. long; earlets in pairs, one-flowered, pale bluish green, alternate. In fields, roadsides or waste places.

Similar in appearance are:

2. VELVET RYE. *Elymus villosus* Muhl. 2½ ft. high; ear 3½ in. long; earlet containing, besides one fertile flower, one or two short, awned, imperfect ones; Awns 1¼ in. long. In woods or on river banks.

3. VIRGINIA RYE. *Elymus virginicus* L. 2½ ft. high; ear 4½ in. Like the last, but awns short, about ½ to ¾ in. long. In marshes along the brooks.

4. CANADA RYE. *Elymus canadensis* L. 4 ft. high; ear 8 in. long. Like foregoing, but awns 1¼ in. long and very rough. On river banks.

5. WHEAT. *Triticum aestivum* L. 3½ ft. high; earlets in fours or fives. There are many cultivars, long-awned and awnless. These include both winter wheat and summer wheat. In fields.

6. BARLEY. *Hordeum vulgare* L. 3 ft. high; ear 3 in. less the long awns; earlet in threes, all fertile. Cultivated.

7. FOXTAIL BARLEY, SQUIRRELTAIL GRASS. *Hordeum jubatum* L. 1½ ft. high, ear 3 in. long. Very slender bristles. Near the coast.

PLATE II

1. QUACKGRASS. *Agropyron repens* (L.) Beauv. 2½ ft. high; ear 5 in. long. Its long, running root-stocks and their vitality are of great trouble to the gardener. Variable, with short awns, or without. Grows everywhere in fields and gardens, along fences and roadsides.

2. SLENDER WHEATGRASS. *Agropyron trachycaulum* (Link) Malte. 1½ ft. high; ear 2½ in. long. Is very similar to above, but has no running roots. In fields.

3. AWNED WHEATGRASS. *Agropyron trachycaulum* (Link) Malte, var. *glaucum* (Pease & Moore) Malte. 2 ft. high, ear 6 in. long. Has awns longer than the glumes, and no running roots. In cultivated ground.

4. CRESTED DOGTAIL. *Cynosurus cristatus* L. 2 ft. high; ear 3 in. long, and spikelets of two kinds. Cultivated for hay.

5. PERENNIAL RYEGRASS. *Lolium perenne* L. 1½ ft. high; ear 5 in. long. Earlets further apart than in Quackgrass, attached edgewise to the stem. The first glume smaller than the earlet. In cultivated grounds and waste places.

6. DARNEL. *Lolium temulentum* L. 3 ft. high; ear 8 in. long. Like the last, but first outside glume larger than the earlet. Seeds said to be poisonous. In grain fields.

7. EASTERN GAMAGRASS. *Tripsacum dactyloides* (L.) L. 6 ft. high; ear 7 in. long, often in pairs or threes, stout; upper half of ear, male flowers, lower half fertile flowers. On streams and in marshes.

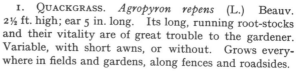

8. HAIR FESCUE. *Festuca capillata* Lam. (or *F. ovina ssp. capillata*). (See Fescue Grasses, pl. VII.)

9. PRICKLEGRASS. *Tragus racemosus* (L.) All. 8 in. high; ear 2½ in. long. Outer scales covered with hooked prickles. In waste places about wharves.

10. DUNE SANDBUR. *Cenchrus tribuloides* L. 1½ ft. high; ear 2 in. long; earlets inside of the prickly burr. On sandy shores.

PLATE III

1. LITTLE BLUESTEM. *Andropogon scoparius* Michx. 3 ft. high; ear 1½ in. long; earlets with a long, slender bristle, their stalks hairy. In sandy fields.

2. BIG BLUESTEM, TURKEYFOOT. *Andropogon gerardii* Vitm. 4½ ft. high; ear 3½ in. long, in pairs.

3. BROOMSEDGE. *Andropogon virginicus* L. 3 ft. high; ear 1 in. long, in pairs; more feathery, but otherwise like last. In fields and along roadsides.

4. BOTTLEBRUSH. *Elymus hystrix* L. (*or hystrix patula*). 3 ft. high; ear 5 in. long; earlets opposite each other on the stem, two-flowered, and with long, slender awns. In rocky woods.

5. POVERTYGRASS. *Aristida dichotoma* Michx. 1 ft. high; ear 3½ in. long. Forked, branching. Resembles 6, only smaller. In sandy soil.

6. THREEAWN. *Aristida longespica* Poir. 14 in. high; ear 5 in. long. In sandy fields.

7. ARROWFEATHER. *Aristida purpurascens* Poir. 2 ft. high; ear 10 in. long. In dry ground.

8. SEABEACH ARISTIDA or NEEDLEGRASS. *Aristida tuberculosa* Nutt. 15 in. high; ear 6 in. long. Like 7, more spreading. On seashore.

9. MATGRASS. *Nardus stricta* L. 10 in. high; ear 2 in. long. Leaves hair-like, in tufts.

PLATE IV

1. *Paspalum setaceum* Michx. 1½ ft. high; ear 2½ in. long, one-sided, single at the top, but short ones protruding from the sheaths. In dry fields.

2. SMOOTH PASPALUM. *Paspalum laeve* Michx. 2 ft. high; ear 4 in. long, one-sided, alternate branching on stem, hairy at the joints, otherwise smooth. In moist fields.

3. CRABGRASS. *Digitaria sanguinalis* (L.) Scop. Upright or creeping, 2 ft. long, spreading; ear 4 in. long, several on end of stalk; leaves hairy, wide. A common weed in cultivated grounds.

4. SMOOTH or SMALL CRABGRASS. *Digitaria ischaemum* (Schreb.) Schreb. 15 in. long; ear 3 in. long; leaves smooth; otherwise like the last.

5. SLENDER CRABGRASS. *Digitaria filiformis* (L.) Koel. Upright, 2½ ft. high, slender. Ear 4 in. long, very narrow; leaves narrow. In sandy fields.

6. *Eleusine indica* (L.) Gaertn. Upright, or spreading in patches, 1 ft. high; ear 2 in. long, earlets many-flowered; leaves smooth. A common weed in waste places.

PLATE V

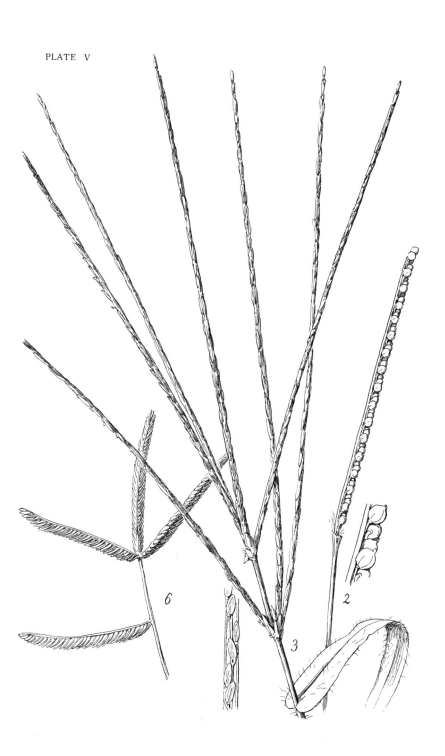

1. REED CANARYGRASS. *Phalaris arundinacea* L. 4 ft. high; ear 6 in. long. Leaves smooth or rough. In marshes or on streams.

2. SPIKE TRISETUM. *Trisetum spicatum* (L.) Richt. 1 ft. high; ear 3 in. long; earlets 3-flowered with 3 bristles; stem and leaves softly hairy. In rocky places.

3. TALL OATGRASS. *Arrhenatherum elatius* (L.) Presl. 3 ft. high; ear 8 in. long; earlets two-flowered, with one bristle; leaves rough, like No. 2, but more open. In fields.

4. LONG-LEAVED RUSHGRASS. *Sporobolus asper* (Michx.) Kunth. 2½ ft. high; ear 7 in. long, partly enclosed in the upper sheath; leaves long. In dry soil.

5. LITTLE RUSHGRASS. *Sporobolus neglectus* Nash. 9 in. high; ear 1½ in. long, partly enclosed in sheath, which is much inflated; leaves short.

6. MATMUHLY. *Muhlenbergia richardsonis* (Trin.) Rydb. 1 ft. high; ear 1½ in. long, not enclosed in sheath; leaves narrow and short.

7. WILD TIMOTHY. *Muhlenbergia glomerata* (Willd.) Trin. (See plate VI and pg. 18.)

Sweet Vernalgrass is sometimes branched at lower part of ear; also Foxtail Millet, and American Beachgrass. The cultivated Ribbon Grass, with white and green striped leaves, is a variety of Reed Canary-grass.

PLATE VI

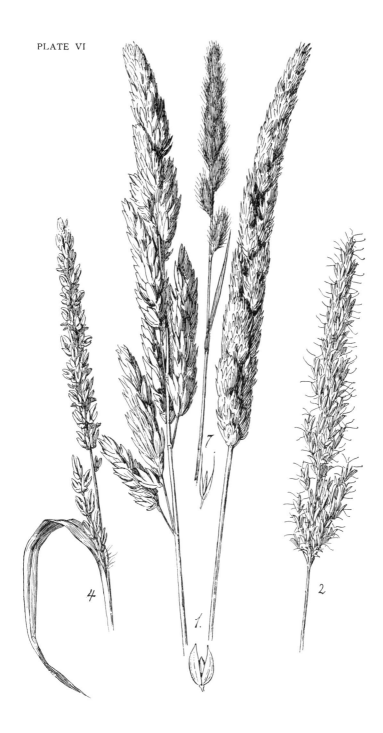

1. ORCHARD GRASS. *Dactylis glomerata* L. 3 ft. high; ear 5 in. long. Much cultivated for fodder, and on shady lawns.

2. SIXWEEKS FESCUE. *Festuca octoflora* Walt. 1 ft. high; ear 3½ in. long, often one-sided and not branched; earlets 7 to 13-flowered; awn as long as scale. In sandy fields.

3. HAIR FESCUE. *Festuca capillata* Lam. (or *F. ovina ssp. capillata*). 1 ft. high; ear 1½ in. long; earlet 4 to 5-flowered, not awned; leaves hairlike, tufted. (See pl. III, fig. 8.)

4. FESCUE. *Festuca myorus* L. 1½ ft. high; ear 4 in. longer than its scale. In waste places and fields.

5. RED FESCUE. *Festuca rubra* L. 2 ft. high; ear 4½ in. long; earlets 3 to 6-flowered; short-awned or only pointed. In fields.

6. SHEEP FESCUE. *Festuca ovina* L. 10 in. high; ear 2½ in. long, one-sided, often unbranched; Earlets 3 to 8-flowered; short awns, about half the length of its scale; leaves tufted, very variable. In fields.

7. WILD TIMOTHY. *Muhlenbergia glomerata* (Willd.) Trin. 2 ft. high; ear 3½ in. long, dense, branch-ears ¾ in. long, oval; earlets awned, no bristle. (See plate VI, fig. 7). In meadows.

8. MUHLY. *Muhlenbergia sylvatica* (Torr.) Torr. 2 ft. high; ear 5 in. long, loose; earlets awned, and with one long bristle. In moist woods.

9. MUHLY. *Muhlenbergia sobolifera* (Muhl.) Trin. 2½ ft. high; ear 4½ in. long; small ears ¾ in. long, very slender; earlets not awned or bristled. In rocky woods.

10. SATINGRASS. *Muhlenbergia mexicana* (L.) Trin. 3 ft. high; ear 4 in. long, small ears 1½ in. long; earlets awned, but not bristled. Resembles No. 8. In swamps.

11. MUHLY. *Muhlenbergia tenuiflora* (Willd.) B.S.P. 2½ ft. high; ear 7 in. long, slender; earlet not awned, but with one long bristle. Resembles No. 9. In rocky woods.

12. NIMBLEWILL. *Muhlenbergia schreberi* Gmel. 2 ft. long, creeping, much branched; ear 5 in. long; earlet sharp pointed and with one long awn. Resembles No. 9. On dry hills and in woods.

13. HAIRGRASS. *Muhlenbergia capillaris* (Lam.) Trin. 2½ ft. high; ear 9 in. long, purplish; earlets single on end of branches. Resembles *Eragrostis pectinacea*, but earlets one-flowered and long-awned. In dry, sandy, rocky soil.

PLATE VII

1. BARNYARD GRASS. *Echinochloa crusgalli* (L.) Beauv. 3 ft. high; ear 10 in. long, small ears in clusters on the stem; earlets with one long awn. In fields and around farms.

2. SALTMARSH COCKSPUR GRASS. *Echinochloa walteri* (Pursh) Heller. 4½ ft. high; ear 12 in. long, brownish purple, small ears alternate on the stem, earlets with two barbed awns of different length, one very long; sheath often hairy.

3. TALL CORDGRASS, SLOUGHGRASS. *Spartina pectinata* Link. 4 ft. high; branch ears 3½ in. long, numerous, on very short stalks, otherwise like No. 5. In swamps and streams.

4. SALTREED GRASS. *Spartina cynosuroides* (L.) Roth. 6 ft. high; branch ears 3 in. long, numerous, on long stalks, otherwise like No. 5. On brackish waters.

5. SALTMEADOW GRASS. *Spartina patens* (Alt.) Muhl. 2 ft. high; branch ears 1½ in. long, few and far apart; leaves very narrow. On salt meadows.

6. SMOOTH or SALTWATER CORDGRASS. *Spartina alterniflora* Loisel. 2 ft. high; branch ears 1½ in. long, few and far apart, ears not spreading. Common along the coast.

See SMOOTH PASPALUM, plate V.

PLATE VIII

Earlets ¼ of an inch long, egg-shaped.

1. MILLET. *Panicum miliaceum* L. 1½ ft. high; ear 7 in. long, broad and bushy, earlets growing upwards; leaves long and broad, one leaf close to ear. Appears like Blunt Mannagrass, pl. XIII. Formerly cultivated for grain. In waste places.

2. BROADLEAVED PANICGRASS. *Panicum latifolium* L. 2 ft. high; ear 4½ in. long, its branches stout, earlets broad; leaves short, heart-shaped, broad and smooth. In wet ground.

3. BOSC'S PANICGRASS. *Panicum boscii* Poir. 1½ ft. high; ear 2½ in. long, branches stout; leaves short, broad, heart-shaped and hairy. In most thickets.

4. SMALLER SEABEACH GRASS. *Panicum amarum* Ell. 2 ft. high; ear 9 in. long, loose, bushy, earlets pale; slender and pointed-leaved to the ear. Sandy shores.

5. SWITCHGRASS. *Panicum virgatum* L. 4 ft. high; ear 12 in. long, branches hairlike, slender, earlets purplish; leaves long and narrow. Moist sandy soil.

6. NORTHERN DROPSEED. *Sporobolus heterolepis* (Gray) Gray. 2 ft. high; ear 7½ in. long; leaves bristle-like, narrow. In dry soil.

7. HOLY GRASS, SENECA or SWEET GRASS. *Hierochloe odorata* (L.) Beauv. 1½ ft. high; ear 3 in. long, one-sided; leaves very short and sweet-scented.

8. ALPINE HOLY GRASS. *Hierochloe alpina* (Sw.) R. & S. Very like the last, but with a bent bristle. On mountains.

Earlets ⅛ of an inch long.

9. DEERTONGUE. *Panicum clandestinum* L. 2¾ ft. long; ear 6 in. long, with many slender clustered branches and many earlets; leaves broad, heart-shaped. Low thickets.

10. WITCHGRASS. *Panicum capillare* L. 1½ ft. high, or creeping; ear 12 in. long, many-fruited, slender branched; leaves middling wide and long. A common weed in fields. Similar in appearance to *Eragrostis*, pl. XIX.; but hairy, and spikelets one-flowered.

11. SLENDER PANICGRASS. *Panicum xanthophysum* Gray. 1½ ft. long; ear 2½ in. long, of few earlets, on short branches which lie close to stem. In dry grounds.

12. SPREADING WITCHGRASS. *Panicum dichotomiflorum* Michx. 1½ ft. high; ear 10 in. long, with many earlets on slender hairlike branches; leaves long and narrow. In wet soil.

13. STARVED PANICGRASS. *Panicum depauperatum* Muhl. 1 ft. high; ear 2 in. long, of few earlets, on stiff branches; leaves long and narrow. In woods and clearings.

14. PANICGRASS. *Panicum oligosanthes* Schult. 15 in. high; ear 2½ in. long. Like the last, but leaves short, upper leaf close to the ear.

15. SAND DROPSEED. *Sporobolus cryptandrus* (Torr.) Gray. 2½ ft. high; ear 8 in. long, many earlets on underside of branches half enclosed in upper narrow leaf. On the shore.

16. MILLET GRASS. *Milium effusum* L. 4 ft. high; ear 6½ in. long, open; few earlets on ends of slender, clustered drooping branches; leaves pointed at both ends. In woods.

Earlets about 1-16 of an inch long.

17. AMERICAN PANICGRASS. *Panicum columbianum* Scribn. 16 in. high; ear 1 in. long; leaves short. In fields and woods.

18. NORTHERN PANICGRASS. *Panicum boreale* Nash. 1½ ft. high; ear 3 in. long, much branched, very slender with few earlets; leaves broad. In wet grounds.

19. EATON'S PANICGRASS. *Panicum spretum* Schult. 2½ ft. high; ear 5 in. long, bushy, with many earlets, crowded; lower leaves broad, upper narrow. On sea shore.

20. WOODLAND WITCHGRASS. *Panicum philadelphicum* Bernh. 16 in. high; ear 6 in. long, open, with few earlets; leaves long and narrow, hairy.

21. PANICGRASS. *Panicum scoparium* Lam. 1 ft. or more high, spreading on the ground; ear 3 in. long, few earlets on hairlike wavy branches; leaves, stem and earlets hairy. Common in dry soil.

22. PANICGRASS. *Panicum nitidum* Lam. 15 in. high; ear 1½ in. long, with few earlets on hairlike spreading branches; leaves narrow. Common in sandy soil.

23. REDTOP PANICGRASS. *Panicum agrostoides* Spreng. 1¾ ft. high; ear 8 in. long, with many earlets, crowded on the lower side of branches; leaves long and narrow. In wet grounds.

24. WARTY PANICGRASS. *Panicum verrucosum* Muhl. 1½ ft. long, slender, spreading; ear 7 in. long, slender, nodding, with few earlets; leaves long and narrow. Wet grounds.

25. MUHLY. *Muhlenbergia uniflora* (Muhl.) Fern. 1 ft. high; ear 6 in. long, with many long-stalked earlets on the slender branches. In wet sandy soil.

PLATE IX

21.

13.

5.

23.

1. BLACK OATGRASS. *Stipa avenacea* L. 2 ft. high; ear 7 in. long, its branches upright and spreading, with black seeds and a twisted and bent awn, 2 in. long. In dry woods.

2. RICEGRASS. *Oryzopsis canadensis* (Poir.) Torr. 1½ ft. high; ear 3½ in. long, contracted; branches and awns upright, awn ½ in. long and twisted. On mountains.

3. BEARDED SHORTHUSK. *Brachyelytrum erectum* Schreb. 2 ft. high; ear 4 in. long branching upwards; awn 1 in. long and straight; leaves broad and pointed at both ends. In moist ground.

4. BLACK MOUNTAIN RICE. *Oryzopsis racemosa* (J. E. Sm.) Ricker. 2 ft. high; ear 7 in. long, awn wavy about ½ in. long; leaves wide. In rocky woods.

5. WHITE MOUNTAIN RICE. *Oryzopsis asperfolia* Michx. 15 in. high; ear 2½ in. long; awn wavy and ½ in. long; leaves medium. In woods.

6. SLENDER MOUNTAIN RICE. *Oryzopsis pungens* (Torr.) Hitchc. 15 in. high; ear 2 in. long; awn very short; leaves hairlike. Among dry rocks.

7. WILD RICE. *Zizania aquatica* L. 6 ft. high; ear 1½ ft. long, its upper half fertile flowers, the lower half sterile flowers, awnless and drooping. In swamps.

To these belong FEATHERGRASS, *Stipa pennata* L., cultivated for ornament, in which the long awn is transformed to a beautiful feather. Rice, *Oryza sativa* L., cultivated southward, is a different tribe.

26

PLATE X

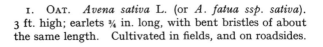

1. OAT. *Avena sativa* L. (or *A. fatua ssp. sativa*). 3 ft. high; earlets ¾ in. long, with bent bristles of about the same length. Cultivated in fields, and on roadsides.

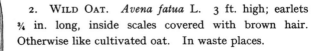

2. WILD OAT. *Avena fatua* L. 3 ft. high; earlets ¾ in. long, inside scales covered with brown hair. Otherwise like cultivated oat. In waste places.

3. PURPLE OAT. *Schizachne purpurascens* (Torr.) Swallen. 1½ ft. high; ear 3½ in. long; the outside glumes purple, and smaller than the earlet. In woodlands.

4. POVERTYGRASS, POVERTY OATGRASS. *Danthonia spicata* (L.) Beauv. 1¾ ft. high; ear 1½ in. long, few earlets; the leaves narrow. Abundant everywhere.

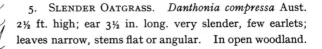

5. SLENDER OATGRASS. *Danthonia compressa* Aust. 2½ ft. high; ear 3½ in. long. very slender, few earlets; leaves narrow, stems flat or angular. In open woodland.

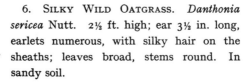

6. SILKY WILD OATGRASS. *Danthonia sericea* Nutt. 2½ ft. high; ear 3½ in. long, earlets numerous, with silky hair on the sheaths; leaves broad, stems round. In sandy soil.

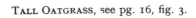

TALL OATGRASS, see pg. 16, fig. 3.

PLATE XI

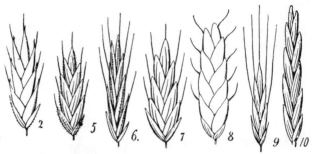

1. SMOOTH CHESS, CHEAT. *Bromus secalinus* L. 2 ft. high; ear 5 in. and earlets ¾ in. long, few, with short awns, drooping. Common in grain fields and near fences.

2. FRINGED BROME. *Bromus ciliatus* L. 3 ft. high, ear 7 in. long, earlets 1 in. long; awns half as long as scales, drooping. More earlets but less wide than in Smooth Chess. In woods.

3. SOFT BROME, DOWNY CHESS. *Bromus tectorum* L. 1¼ ft. high; ear 4 in. long, earlet ¾ in. long, with awns of the same length, earlets and sheath downy, drooping. In fields.

4. BARREN BROME GRASS. *Bromus sterilis* L. 1½ ft. high; ear 7 in. long, earlets flattened; awns 1 in. long, drooping. Waste grounds and river banks.

5. WILD CHESS. *Bromus kalmii* Gray. 2½ ft. high; ear 4 in. long, earlets ¾ in. long; awns short, drooping. In woods.

6. FRINGED BROME. *Bromus ciliatus* L. 4 ft. high, slender; ear 9 in. long, earlets 1¼ in. long; awns as long as glumes; leaves hairy. In waste places.

7. HAIRY CHESS. *Bromus commutatus* Schrad. 2 ft. high; ear 5 in. long, earlets upright, awns as long as the shining scales. In fields and near fences.

8. CORN BROME. *Bromus squarrosus* L. 1 ft. high; ear 4 in., nodding; awns as long as the shining scales, bending outward; leaves very narrow, hairy. Near wharves.

9. GREAT FESCUE. *Festuca gigantea* (L.) Vill. 3 ft. high; ear 9 in. long, earlet ¾ in. with awn of the same length, upright. Resembles No. 7. In waste grounds.

10. SMOOTH or AWNLESS BROME. *Bromus inermis* Leyss. 3 ft. high; ear 6 in. long, earlets awnless, 1¼ in. long. (Drawing of ear reduced.) Cultivated for hay.

30

PLATE XII

1.

7.

10.

1. REEDGRASS. *Calamagrostis cinnoides* (Muhl.) Bart. 4 ft. high; ear 5 in. long, white silky hair in earlets longer on one side than on the other. Common in ditches and swamps.

2. PICKERING'S REEDGRASS. *Calamagrostis pickeringii* Gray. 15 in. high; ear 3½ in. long, open during flowering; short silky hair on one side only. On mountains.

3. NORTHERN REEDGRASS. *Calamagrostis inexpansa* Gray. 2½ ft. high; ear 6 in. long; silky hair nearly equal in length on both sides. North-westward.

4. NARROW REEDGRASS. *Calamagrostis neglecta* (Ehrh.) Gaertn. 2 ft. high; ear 3¾ in. long; silky hairs about half the length of spikelet and nearly even; leaves narrow. Mountains northward. See also *Calamagrostis canadensis, ssp. scabra,* pg. 38.

5. PRAIRIE WEDGEGRASS. *Sphenopholis obtusata* (Michx.) Scribn. 1¼ ft. high; ear 4 in. long, two-flowered; branches of ear very short, showing stem between the clusters. In dry soil.

6. SHINING WEDGEGRASS. *Sphenopholis nitida* (Bieler) Scribn. 2 ft. high; ear 5 in. long, slender, open. Hilly woods.

8.

7. *Sorghum nutans* (L.) Gray (or *Sorghastrum nutans*). 6 ft. high; ear 8 in. long, rather open; earlets in pairs, yellowish brown; leaves broad. In dry fields.

Closely related to No. 7 are Broom Corn, Guinea Corn, Indian Millet, *Sorghum vulgare* Pers. (Sorghum) and *halepense* (L.) Pers. (Johnson Grass). Spikelets with two sterile flowers instead of the feathers in No. 7. Cultivated southward. Sugar Cane, *Saccharum officinarum* L., also belongs here.

9

8. REED. *Phragmites communis* Trin. 8 ft. high; ear 9 in. long, very broad, long, silky, hairy, several-flowered; leaves 2 in. wide. On the borders of ponds and swamps.

10.

9. SLENDER MANNAGRASS. *Glyceria melicaria* (Michx.) Hubb. 2½ ft. high; ear 9 in. long, nodding, very slender, with few many-flowered earlets. In wet woods.

11.

32

PLATE XIII

1.

9.

11.

10.

Continued from page 32.

10. BLUNT MANNAGRASS. *Glyceria obtusa* (Muhl.) Trin. 2 ft. high; ear 5 in. long. On the edge of ditches and swamps.

See also Millet, pg. 22, No. 1; ear similar, but earlets one-flowered.

11. SEASHORE SALTGRASS. *Distichlis spicata* (L.) Greene. 1 ft. high; ear 1½ in. long; leaves narrow. Salt marshes.

NOTE:—Ears resembling Slender Mannagrass are Nodding Fescue, Weak Speargrass, and Wood Bluegrass, pp. 46, 48, and some Panic-grasses, pl. IX. Ears resembling Reedgrass, besides Nos. 1 to 8, are the Smaller Seabeach Grass, and Millet, pl. IX.

1. REDTOP. *Agrostis gigantea* Roth (or *A. alba*). 20 in. high; ear 6 in. long, greenish, purplish, or brownish; earlets ⅛ in., usually white inside; scales carmine red with a green keel; very variable in size and appearance. Much cultivated. Ear contracted after flowering, and ligule (skinny piece which joins the leaf to the stem) long and pointed. On roadsides and in meadows.

COLONIAL BENT. *Agrostis tenuis* Sibth. Ear spreading after flowering; ligule short and blunt. In low meadows and pastures.

2. VELVET BENT. *Agrostis canina* L. 1½ ft. high; ear 4 in. long, earlet with a small, bent bristle; lower half of branches bare, straight, and upper half crowded with earlets. On roadsides and in meadows.

3. BENTGRASS. *Agrostis borealis* Hartm. 15 in. high; ear 3¾ in. long; earlet with small bristle, but branches three-fourths their length bare, wavy, and one-fourth sparingly beset with earlets. On high mountains and northward.

34

PLATE XIV

4. AUTUMN BENT. *Agrostis perennans* (Walt.) Tuckerm. 1¼ in. high; ear 6 in. long, no bristle, branches hairlike and branching more than half their length, earlets 1-16 in. long. In woods.

5. HAIRGRASS. *Agrostis scabra* Willd. 2 ft. high; ear 15 in. long, very open, purplish, branches hairlike, rough, with earlets at their tips only, 1-16 in. long. In cleared woodlands.

6. BENTGRASS. *Agrostis borealis* Hartm. 1 ft. high; ear 6 in. long; like a stout Autumn Bent with earlets of double size. In the mountains and northward.

7. BENTGRASS. *Agrostis spica-venti* L. 1½ ft. high; ear 6 in. long; like Hairgrass; spikelets ⅛ in. long and with a long bristle. Near the shore.

NOTE:—Ears resembling Colonial Bent and Redtop are Bentgrass, pl. xv, Bluejoint, pl. xvi.
　　Ears resembling Autumn Bent are Hairgrass, pl. xv, Muhly, pg. 24, Hairgrass, pg. 18, the greater part of the Panicgrasses, pl. ix, some of the *Eragrostis*, pl. xix, and *Deschampsia*, pl. xvii.

PLATE XV

5.

1.   BLUEJOINT.   *Calamagrostis canadensis* (Michx.) Beauv.   4 ft. high; ear 6 in. long; the white silky hair on one side, inside of the spikelet, half as long as on the other.   Valued as fodder grass.   In swamps and border of rivers.

2.   *Calamagrostis canadensis* (Mx.) Beauv., *ssp. scabra* (Presl.) Hitch.   3 ft. high; ear 4 in. long, the white silky hair of even length, about ¾ the length of the spikelet. Less spreading than No. 1.   In mountain swamps.

3. RICE CUTGRASS.   *Leersia oryzoides* (L.) Swartz. 2½ ft. high; ear 7 in. long, earlets ¼ in. long; leaves very rough.   In wet woody swamps.

4. WHITEGRASS.   *Leersia virginica* Willd.   2   ft. high; ear 5 in. long, earlets ⅛ in. long; leaves short; stems slender; otherwise like No. 3.   In wet woods.

5.   PURPLE SANDGRASS.   *Triplasis purpurea* (Walt.) Chapm.   2 ft. high; ear 2 in. long; leaves short.   On sea beaches.   See pl. XVII, fig. 6.

PLATE XVI

3.   1.

1.   VELVET GRASS. *Holcus lanatus* L.   2½ ft. high; ear 4 in. long, whitish velvety all over, earlets two-flowered.   In fields and meadows.

2.   SILVER HAIRGRASS. *Aira caryophillea* L.   8 in. long; earlets ⅛ in. long, two-flowered, with two bristles, branches in pairs, ear shining silvery; leaves bristle-like. In fields.

3.   TUFTED HAIRGRASS. *Deschampsia caespitosa* (L.) Beauv.   3 ft. high; ear 6 in. long earlets two-flowered with two short bristles; branches in threes or fours; leaves flat.   In wet grounds.

4.   CRINKLED HAIRGRASS. *Deschampsia flexuosa* (L.) Trin.   1½ ft. high; ear 5 in. long, earlet ¼ in. long, two-flowered, with two long bent bristles, branches in pairs; leaves bristle-like.   In dry soil.

5.   MOUNTAIN HAIRGRASS. *Deschampsia atropurpurea* (Wahl.) Scheele.   1 ft. high; ear 1½ in. long, purple earlets ¼ in. long, with two short bent awns, branches single or double, few; leaves flat.   White Mountains and northward.

6.   PURPLE SANDGRASS. *Triplasis purpurea* (Walt.) Chapm. See pg. 38, No. 5.

NOTE:—Ears resembling Crinkled Hairgrass are Bentgrass, pg. 34, Bentgrass, pg. 36.

PLATE XVII

1. SHARPSCALED MANNAGRASS. *Glyceria acutiflora* Torr. 2 ft. high; stems flat, half creeping below: ear 9 in. long, simple, with few branches very far apart, fertile scales pointed and long. In water covered places.

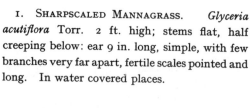 

2. EASTERN MANNAGRASS. *Glyceria septentrionalis* Hitchc. 3½ ft. long; stems flat; ear 1 ft. long, fertile scales of earlet blunt; short, otherwise like last.

3. MEADOW FESCUE. *Festuca elatior* L. 3½ ft. high; ear 9 in. long; leaves long and medium wide. In cultivated ground, or roadsides.

4. ALKALIGRASS. *Puccinellia maritima* (Huds.) Parl. 1½ ft. high; ear 4 in. long; resembles the last, but leaves are short and very narrow. In salt marshes.

5. SALTMEADOW GRASS. *Leptochloa fascicularis* (Lam.) Gray. 2 ft. high, grows in tufts; ear 8 in. long. Like Meadow Fescue but ear more slender, earlets few and farther apart; leaves long and narrow; flowering scales with two short teeth and short awn. In brackish marshes.

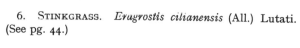

6. STINKGRASS. *Eragrostis cilianensis* (All.) Lutati. (See pg. 44.)

42

PLATE XVIII

3

6

1.

1. STINKGRASS. *Eragrostis cilianensis* (All.) Lutati. 1½ ft. high; ear 4 in. long, earlets flat, many-flowered crowded into a close ear, upright. (See pl. XVIII, fig. 6.) In sandy, waste places.

2. LOVEGRASS. *Eragrostis reptans* (Michx.) Nees. 9 in. long; creeping upright branches about 3 in. long, sterile and fertile spikelets on different plants, sterile scales pointed. On gravely river banks.

3. LOW LOVEGRASS. *Eragrostis poaeoides* Beauv. 15 in. high; ear 3½ in. long; like Stinkgrass, but ear open with few earlets, two or four on lower branch. Cultivated ground and waste places.

4. PURSH or CAROLINA LOVEGRASS. *Eragrostis pectinacea* (Michx.) Nees. 1 ft. high, creeping below, tufted; ear open, 6 in. long, earlets on both sides of branches; leaves narrow. On dry ground.

5. PURPLE LOVEGRASS. *Eragrostis spectabilis* (Pursh) Steud. 2 ft. high; ear 15 in. long, earlets mostly on lower side of branches. On dry soil.

6. INDIA LOVEGRASS. *Eragrostis pilosa* (L.) Beauv. 1 ft. high; ear 4 in. long. On cultivated grounds.

7. LACEGRASS. *Eragrostis capillaris* (L.) Nees 1 ft. high; ear 10 in. long; stems hairlike.

NOTE:—Ears resembling Pursh or Carolina Lovegrass are *Eragrostis capillaris* and *pilosa*, Witchgrass and Dropseeds, pp. 22, 23.

PLATE XIX

6

1. ANNUAL BLUEGRASS, SPEARGRASS. *Poa annua* L. Less than 1 ft. high; ear 2 in. long, one-sided; stems flattened, branches spreading, earlets short-stalked, crowded. Cultivated and waste ground.

2. CANADA BLUEGRASS. *Poa compressa* L. 1¼ ft. high; ear 4 in. long; branches mostly in pairs, pointed upwards; leaves pale; stem very flat and broad, dark blue-green. On roadsides.

3. KENTUCKY BLUEGRASS. *Poa pratensis* L. 2½ ft. high; ear 5 in. long; stems round, earlets ¼ in. long, crowded on end-half of branches, almost sessile. Much cultivated.

4. ROUGH BLUEGRASS. *Poa trivialis* L. 2 ft. high; ear 5 in. long, earlet ⅛ in. long, stemmed and less crowded on three-quarters of end of branches. In moist meadows.

5. GROVE MEADOWGRASS. *Poa alsodes* Gray. 1½ ft. high; ear 5 in. long, slender, open, earlets scattered, mostly long-stemmed, ¼ in. long. In shady woods.

6. FOWL BLUEGRASS. *Poa palustris* L. 3½ ft. high; ear 9 in. long, earlets 3-16 in. long on underside of branches, all short-stalked. In moist meadows.

This and No. 5 resemble *Agrostis gigantea*, but have several-flowered earlets.

7. ALKALIGRASS. *Puccinellia distans* (L.) Parl. 1½ ft. high; ear 4½ in. long, earlets crowded on upper half of branches; leaves short and narrow. On salt marshes.

8. GLAUCOUS SPEARGRASS. *Poa glauca* Vahl. 1½ ft. high; ear 2 in. long, branches upright, rough, with single earlets at their ends, one-sided. White Mountains.

9. ALPINE SPEARGRASS. *Poa laxa* Haenke. 1 ft. high; ear 2 in. long. Like the last, but branches smooth. White Mountains and northward.

10. WOOD BLUEGRASS. *Poa nemoralis* L. 1½ ft. high; ear 3½ in. long. Like Weak Speargrass, but branches shorter, beset with earlets more than half their length. Mountains northward.

Nos. 8 and 9 resemble 1, but earlets upright, ears one-sided.

PLATE XX

Continued from page 46.

11. WEAK SPEARGRASS. *Poa languida* Hitchc. 1½ ft. high; ears 4 in. long. Like last, but branches upright, one-sided, nodding, beset with earlets less than half their length, and leaves longer. In woods.

12. NODDING FESCUE. *Festuca obtusa* Bieh. 2½ ft. high; ear 6 in. long, very slender and open, earlets far apart; leaves long, dark green. In rocky woods.

Nos. 10, 11, 12, resemble Slender Mannagrass, pl. XIII, fig. 9, but more slender and with fewer spikelets.

1. QUAKING GRASS. *Briza media* L. 1½ ft. high; ear 3 in. long, earlets round, heart-shaped, flat, drooping, branches in pairs. In fields and meadows.

2. RATTLESNAKE MANNAGRASS. *Glyceria canadensis* (Michx.) Trin. 2½ ft. high; ear 8 in. long, earlets ¼ to ½ in. long, flat, oblong, drooping, branches in threes or more. In swamps.

3. MANNAGRASS. *Glyceria canadensis*, var. *laxa* (Scribn.) Hitchc. 3 ft. high; ear 8 in. long, earlets ⅛ in. long, upright or spreading, branches in pairs. In wet soil.

4. FOWL or NERVED MANNAGRASS. *Glyceria striata* (Lam.) Hitchc. 2 ft. high; ear 5 in. long, branches spreading and drooping, earlets ⅛ in. long, first pair and flowering scales ribbed and rounded. In marshes.

5. PALE MANNAGRASS. *Puccinellia pallida* (Torr.) R. T. Clausen (or *Glyceria pallida*). 2 ft. high, pale green; ear 4 in. long, earlet ¼ in. long. Similar to Fowl Mannagrass, except less drooping, narrower leaves and blunt scales.

6. AMERICAN MANNAGRASS. *Glyceria grandis* S. Wats (or *Glyceria maxima*, *ssp. grandis*). 4 ft. high; ear 1 ft. long, stout, upright, earlets ¼ in. long, first pair of scales pointed, the others strongly ribbed; leaves wide and long. In wet ground.

48

PLATE XXI

1. DROOPING WOODREED.   *Cinna latifolia* (Trev.) Griseb.   3 ft. high; ear 7½ in. long, drooping, open.   The two outer scales of the spikelet of nearly the same size. In damp woods.

 2. STOUT WOODREED.   *Cinna arundinacea* L.   3½ ft. high; ear 9 in. long, stout, drooping, spreading in flowering time, sometimes bushy.   The two outer scales of the spikelet of unequal size.   In wet woodlands.

There are yet to mention with no North American relations:

MAIZE, INDIAN CORN.   *Zea mays* L.   10 ft. high, with several fertile ears in the axils of the lower leaves and a sterile ear on the top of the stem; stems solid.   Originally from America, probably the Mexican plateau.   Cultivated.

PAMPASGRASS.   *Cortaderia selloana* (Schult.) Aschers & Graebn. 10 ft. high, from a large tuft of long, curved leaves; ear large, silvery-silky, fertile and sterile flowers on separate plants.   Cultivated in gardens.

PLATE XXII

1.

KEY TO THE SEDGE FAMILY, *Cyperaceae.*

Spikes or spikelets all of one kind of flowers; all perfect.
Many-flowered spikelets:

    flat spikelets, flowers in two rows.   .   CYPERUS.   DULICHIUM
    rounded spikelets, flowers in several rows all around stem:
      no leaves, one spikelet at end of stem.

                          ELEOCHARIS.   SCIRPUS
      leaf⌡, one or several spikelets in sessile clusters.

        SCIRPUS.   RHYNCHOSPORA.   FUIRENA.   HEMICARPHA
    clustered spikelets on umbrella-like spreading stemlets;
      plant tall. .   .   .   . SCIRPUS
    single spikelets on umbrella-like spreading stemlets;
      plant small.   .   .   . BULBOSTYLIS.   FIMBRISTYLIS.
Numerous few-flowered spikelets in head-like clusters at end of stem:
    with long, silky hair.   .   .   .   . ERIOPHORUM
    no silky hairs; often several clusters, distant, on stem.

                      RYNCHOSPORA.   CLADIUM

Spikes of two kinds of flowers on the same or separate spikes.
Upper spikes not fertile, lower spikes fertile, or upper part of the
    same spike sterile and lower part fertile; also upper
    part fertile and lower part sterile:
    fruits naked .   .   .   . SCLERIA
    fruits enclosed in a pouch or bag   .   .   .   . CAREX

SEDGE FAMILY: *Cyperaceae.*

I. GALINGALE. UMBRELLA SEDGE.
Cyperus.

1. *Cyperus diandrus* Torr. 6 in. high; spikelets pale green with purplish edges, or purplish, very flat and thin; seed gray. In low grounds.

2. *Cyperus rivularis* Kunth. 7 in. high; spikelets brown and more firm, otherwise like *C. diandrus*; seed brown. Edges of streams and ponds.

3. *Cyperus flavescens* L. 7 in. high; spikelets straw yellow, narrow; seed black; otherwise like *C. diandrus*. Low grounds.

4. *Cyperus filicinus* Vahl. 10 in. high; spikelets over 1 in. long, loosely clustered, yellowish brown. In brackish marshes.

5. *Cyperus fuscus* L. 1 ft. high; spikelets brown with a green keel, less than ½ in. long. Near shore.

6. *Cyperus dentatus* Torr. 14 in. high; spikelets reddish brown, ¾ in. long. Sandy swamps.

───────────

7. *Cyperus filiculmis* Vahl. 1 ft. high; spikelets in close, round heads, green; stems wire-like. In dry fields.

8. *Cyperus aristatus* (Am. Authors). 4 in. high; spikelets light brown in single heads, awned; stems hair-like. On sandy shores.

9. *Cyperus houghtonii* Torr. 1½ ft. high; spikelets chestnut brown, with several stemmed heads; otherwise like *C. filiculmis*. In sandy soil.

10. *Cyperus grayii* Torr. 9 in. high; spikelets greenish-chestnut colored, loose in many long-stemmed heads; leaves bristle-shaped, stems thread-like. On barren sands.

───────────

11. YELLOW NUTSEDGE or NUTGRASS. *Cyperus esculentus* L. 1½ ft. high; stems stout; spikelets numerous, growing from the sides of their stems, flat; spikes

and leaves yellowish green; roots with small tubers; seed narrow, oblong, blunt.   In wet fields on brooks.

12. *Cyperus erythrorhizos* Muhl.   2 ft. high, more or less; spikelets bright chestnut; otherwise like *C. esculentus*; seed egg-shaped.   On edge of rivers.

13. *Cyperus strigosus* L.   2 ft. high; spikelets straw-colored, flat, from ¼ to 1 in. long; seed narrow, oblong, pointed.   Very variable; grows from bulbs.   In wet grounds and fields.

14. *Cyperus odoratus* L.   1½ ft. high; spikelets very narrow, roundish, dull brown.   In marshes.

15. *Cyperus engelmanii* Steud.   2 ft. high; spikelets very narrow and round, greenish-brown.   In wet soil.

---

16. THREEWAY SEDGE. *Dulichium arundinaceum* (L.) Britt.   2 ft. high; leaves in three regular rows along the whole length of the round stem; in their axils grows the stemlet with the roundish spikelets.   On ponds and in swamps.

NOTE:—Very similar to each other in the appearance of the ear are Nos. 1 to 6, 7 to 10, and 11 to 15.

II. SPIKERUSH. *Eleocharis.*

1. *Eleocharis equisetoides* (Ell.) Torr.   2½ ft. high; spikes many-flowered, not wider than stem; stem knotted or jointed.   In water.

2. *Eleocharis robbinsii* Oakes.   1½ ft. long; spikes not wider than stem, few-flowered; stems not jointed, with hair-like branches at the bottom.   In shallow water.

PLATE XXIII

Spikes wider than stem.

3. *Eleocharis palustris* (L.) R. & S. 3 ft. high; spike lance-shaped with rounded point: stem stout. In ponds and marshes.

4. *Eleocharis rostellata* (Torr.) Torr. 3 ft. high; spike lance-shaped, pointed; stem slender, wiry. In marsh and wet meadows.

5. *Eleocharis tuberculosa* (Michx.) R. & S. 16 in. high; spike egg-shaped; stem slender, but stiff. In wet soil.

6. *Eleocharis compressa* Sulliv. 16 in. high; spike roundish, egg-shaped; stem flat. In wet soil.

7. *Eleocharis melanocarpa* Torr. 15 in. high; spike oblong, blunt; stem flat. In wet sandy soil.

8. *Eleocharis tenuis* (Willd.) Schult. 12 in. high; spike narrow, oblong; stems hairlike, 4-angled. In wet soil.

9. *Eleocharis ovata* (Roth) R. & S. 9 in. high; spike egg-shaped, rounded; stem thread-like. In wet grounds.

10. *Eleocharis engelmannii* Stend. 9 in. high; spike lance-shaped, pointed; stem thread-like. Wet soil.

11. *Eleocharis intermedia* (Muhl.) Schult. 8 in. high; spike oblong, egg-shaped, small; stem hair-like. In marshes.

12. *Eleocharis acicularis* (L.) R. & S. 5 in. high; spike narrow, egg-shaped; stem finely hairlike. In wet soil.

13. *Eleocharis olivacea* Torr. 2½ in. high; spike egg-shaped, brown; stems slender, bright green. In wet soil.

NOTE:—All this group and Nos. 1 to 5 of the next group, *Scirpus*, are very similar in the appearance of the ear.

PLATE XXIV

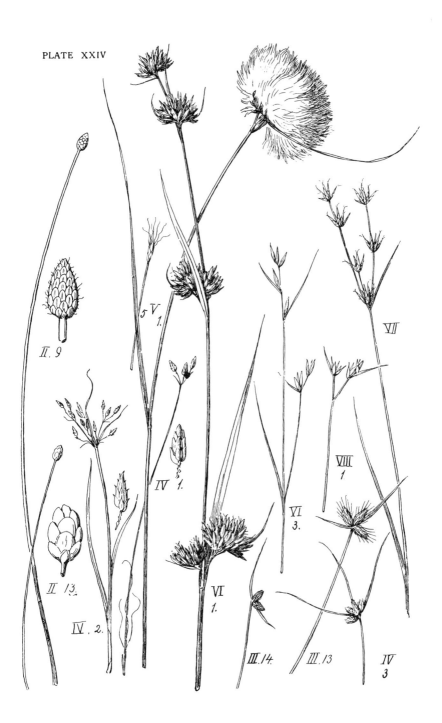

II. 9

5 V₁.

IV 1.

II 13.

IV. 2.

VI 1.

III.14. *III.13.*

VI 3.

VIII 1

VII

IV 3

III. BULRUSH. *Scirpus.*

Spikes single at end of stem.

1. LITTLE SPIKERUSH. *Eleocharis parvula* (R. & S.) Link. 1½ in. high; stem hair-like, flattened, no leaves; spike oblong, egg-shaped, and pale green; otherwise like *Eleocharis olivacea.* In mud on salt marshes.

2. STARVED SPIKERUSH. *Eleocharis pauciflora* (Lightf.) Link. 6 in. high; stem slender, triangular, leafless; scales pointed, bristly. In wet grounds.

3. *Scirpus clintonii* Gray. 10 in. high; resembles an *Eleocharis* with one narrow leaf and a short bract under the spike; stem slender, triangular. In dry fields.

4. *Scirpus verecundus* Fern. 12 in. high; like *S. clintonii,* but scales sharp-pointed. In woods.

5. *Scirpus subterminalis* Torr. 2½ ft. long; stem knotted; leaf 12 in. long; spike oblong, with a longer bract; otherwise like *S. clintonii.* In ponds.

Several sessile, clustered spikes.
One long subtending leaf.

6. *Scirpus hallii* Gray. 9 in. high; stem bluntly triangular; spikelets one or two, clustered, sessile, oblong, cylindrical; one hair-like leaf. In wet soil.

7. *Scirpus purshianus* Fern. 1¼ ft. high; stem round; spikelets in threes or more, egg-shaped, scales egg-shaped; rarely with one short leaf. In wet soil.

8. *Scirpus smithii* Gray. 8 in. high; stems round, very slender; spikelets in threes or more, scales reversed egg-shaped; rarely with one short leaf. In wet places.

9. CHAIRMAKER'S RUSH. *Scirpus americanus* (Am. Authors). 2½ ft. high; stem sharply triangular, two sides concave, one flat; spikelets oblong, egg-shaped, several scales with awns. In fresh and brackish swamps.

10. OLNEY'S RUSH. *Scirpus olneyi* Gray. 4 ft. high; stem sharply triangular, sides concave; spikelets oblong, egg-shaped, many scales with very short awn. Salt marshes.

11. *Scirpus torreyi* Olney. 3 ft. high; stem sharply triangular; spikelets oblong, few scales, long egg-shaped. In swamps.

58

12. *Scirpus robustus* Pursh. 3½ ft. high; stem sharply triangular, sides flat; spikelets oblong, egg-shaped, many in the often compound cluster, scales egg-shaped with an awn.   In salt marshes.

13. UMBRELLA GRASS. *Fuirena squarrosa* Michx. 12 in. high; stem tufted; spikelets ½ in. long in clusters of threes or more, scales with long awns.   In wet meadows.

14. *Hemicarpha micrantha* (Vahl) Pax. 3 ft. high; stems flattened, in tufts; spikelets ⅛ in. long, egg-shaped on sides of stems.   In moist sandy soil.

Clusters stemmed.

15. WOOLGRASS. *Scirpus cyperinus* (L.) Kunth. 4 ft. high; stem slightly triangular, almost round; spikelets ¼ in. long, on second branches, oblong egg-shaped, mostly in threes or fives, very woolly.   In wet grounds.

16. *Scirpus polyphyllus* Vahl. 3 ft. high; stem sharply triangular; spikelets ⅛ in. long, egg-shaped, mostly in threes on second branches.   In wet woods.

17. *Scirpus microcarpus* Presl. 4 ft. high; stem stout; spikelets less than ¼ in. long, oblong egg-shaped, on second branches in threes or fives.   In wet grounds.

18. DARK GREEN BULRUSH. *Scirpus atrovirens* Willd. 3 ft. high; stem triangular, slender; spikelets oblong, six or more in each cluster on first or short second branches. In swamps.

19. *Scirpus expansus* Fern. 5 ft. high; stem triangular, stout; spikelets ¼ in. long, on second branches in threes, oblong.   In swamps.

20. RIVER BULRUSH. *Scirpus fluviatilis* (Torr.) Gray. 4½ ft. high; stem sharply triangular, with flat sides; spikelets ¾ in. long, oblong, cylindrical, on first branches; scales with an awn.

21. SOFTSTEM or GREAT BULRUSH. *Scirpus validus* Vahl. 6 ft. high; stem stout, sometimes 1 in. thick, round; spikelets ¼ in. long, single or in threes or fours in clusters on the second branches, long, egg-shaped, pointed; scales reversed egg-shaped.

NOTE:—Nos. 6 to 14 and 15 to 21 are very similar in the appearance of the ear.

59

IV. *Bulbostylis.*

1. HAIR RUSH. *Bulbostylis capillaris* (L.) C. B. Clarke. 6 in. high; stems and leaves hair-like; spikelets slightly 4-angled, few at end of stem; seed triangular. In moist or dry soil, in tufts.

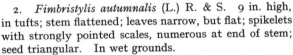

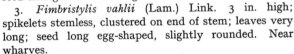

2. *Fimbristylis autumnalis* (L.) R. & S. 9 in. high, in tufts; stem flattened; leaves narrow, but flat; spikelets with strongly pointed scales, numerous at end of stem; seed triangular. In wet grounds.

3. *Fimbristylis vahlii* (Lam.) Link. 3 in. high; spikelets stemless, clustered on end of stem; leaves very long; seed long egg-shaped, slightly rounded. Near wharves.

4. *Rhynchospora scirpoides* Griseb. 9 in. high; seed round and flattened like a lens; otherwise like *F. autumnalis*.

NOTE:—All of above similar in the appearance of the ear.

V. COTTONGRASS. *Eriophorum.*

1. TAWNY or BUTTON COTTONGRASS. *Eriophorum virginicum* L. 3 ft. high; with white or brownish heads; stem leafy. In bogs.

2. SLENDER COTTONGRASS. *Eriophorum gracile* W. D. J. Koch. 1½ ft. high; stems slender, leafy, with several white heads on long slender stemlets, drooping. In swamps.

3. THINLEAVED COTTONGRASS. *Eriophorum viridicarinatum* (Engelm.) Fern. 2½ ft. high; stem stiff, leafy, heads numerous; otherwise like the last.

4. HARE'S TAIL. *Eriophorum spissum* Fern. 1 ft. high; with single heads; two sheaths, but no leaves.

5. ALPINE COTTONGRASS. *Eriophorum alpinum* L. (or *Scirpus hudsonianus*). 8 in. high; heads single, small, with few white hairs; leaves ¾ in. long. In the mountains.

NOTE:—All of above similar in the appearance of the ear.

PLATE XXV

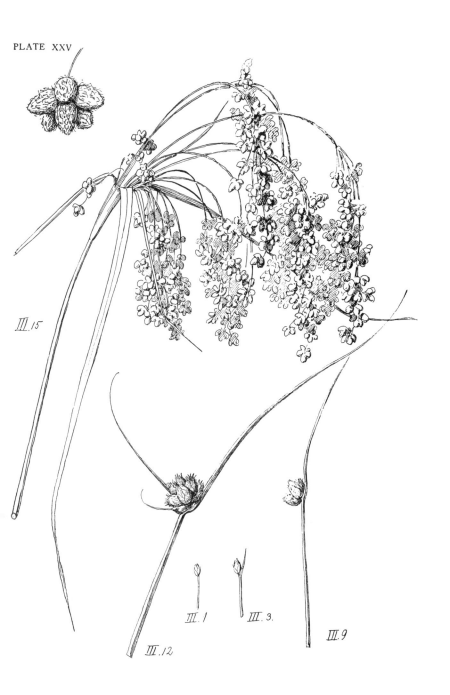

III.15

III.1

III.3.

III.12

III.9

VI. BEAKRUSH. *Rhynchospora.*

1. CLUSTERED BEAKRUSH. *Rhynchospora glomerata* (L.) Vahl. 2 ft. high; spikelets purplish brown, in distant short-stemmed clusters on upper half of the stem. In moist grounds.

2. BROWNISH BEAKRUSH. *Rhynchospora fusca* (L.) Ait. 1 ft. high; two or three clusters on the end of stem, the lower long-stemmed, brown. In bogs.

3. CAPILLARY BEAKRUSH. *Rhynchospora capillacea* Torr. 1 ft. high; stem and leaves hair-like, with few loose chestnut brown spikelets on end of stems. In bogs.

4. WHITE BEAKRUSH. *Rhynchospora alba* (L.) Vahl. 1 ft. high; spikelets white, one or two clusters on end of stem. In bogs.

VII. *Cladium.*

1. TWIGRUSH. *Cladium mariscoides* (Muhl.) Torr. 2½ ft. high, with a few long-stemmed, small, loose clusters on end of stem or from axils of leaves. In marshes.

VIII. NUTRUSH. *Scleria.*

1. NUTRUSH. *Scleria reticularis* Michx. 1¾ ft. high; stem slender, upright, 3-angled; spikelets few in loose clusters on end of stem and axils of leaves; seed globular, white, ribbed. In meadows.

2. NUTRUSH. *Scleria pauciflora* Muhl. 1½ ft. high; stem 3-angled; spikelets very few; seed thimble-shaped, white, with little warts like dots, which are longer at lower end. In dry soil.

3. NUTRUSH. *Scleria verticillata* Muhl. 14 in. high; stem hairlike, 3-angled; spikelets in threes or fours, distant, small, clusters at the upper part of stem; seed globular, white, with horizontal elevated lines. In moist meadows.

NOTE:—All of the *Rynchospora, Cladium* and *Scleria* are similar to each other in the appearance of the ear.

KEY TO THE SEDGES PROPER. *Carex.*

Two kinds of spikes on same plant; upper spike or spikes narrow, sterile, lower spikes fertile; or, sometimes, upper spike partly fertile. Seed 3-angled, thick.

Seed pouch with a **long beak:**
    Seed pouch ½ in. or more in length:
        fertile spike loose-flowered, -   -   -   -   Nos. 1, 2, 3
                globular,   -   -   -   -   -   4, 5
                oblong cylindrical, -   -   -   -   6, 7

    Seed pouch between ½ and ¼ in. in length:
        fertile spike oblong cylindrical, -   -   -   -   8 to 17
                few-flowered -   -   -   -   -   18

    Seed pouch between ¼ and ⅛ in. in length:
        fertile spike globular oblong, -   -   -   -   19 to 22
                oblong,   -   -   -   -   -   23 to 29
                cylindrical,   -   -   -   -   30 to 36

    Seed pouch ⅛ in. or less in length:
        fertile spike cylindrical,   -   -   -   -   37 to 40
                oblong globular,   -   -   -   41 to 47

Seed pouch with **no beak,** or a very short one;
    fertile spike 1 in. or more in length,
            ¼ in. or more thick,   -   -   .   -   48 to 51
            ¼ in. or less thick,   -   -   -   52 to 57

    fertile spike more than ½ in. and less than 1 in. in length,
            ¼ in. or more thick,   -   -   -   58 to 61
            between ¼ and ⅛ in. thick   -   -   62 to 75
            ⅛ in. thick or less,   -   -   -   76 to 78
    fertile spike less than ½ in. in length,   -   -   79 to 83

Plants with one kind of spikes, the fertile and sterile flowers separate. They may be either all fertile at the base and sterile at the top, or sterile at the base and fertile at the top on the same spike; or sometimes sterile and fertile flowers mixed. Seed lentil-shaped, flat.

    Spike sterile at the top and fertile below
        of few-flowered, single head-like clusters,   -   -   -   84 to 87
        yellowish or brownish, aggregated on end of stem,   -   88 to 93
        yellowish, simple clusters more or less interrupted,   -   94 to 100

    Spike fertile at the top and sterile below
        seed pouch wingless,   -   -   -   -   -   101 to 107
        seed pouch with wing-like edge,   -   -   -   108 to 118

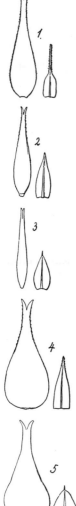

IX. SEDGE. *Carex.*

1. *Carex folliculata* L. 2½ ft. long; yellowish green, stem upright or reclining; two to four fertile spikes 1¼ in. long, loose, roundish egg-shaped, far apart, the lower long-stalked, nodding. In swamps.

2. *Carex michauxiana* Boeckl. 1½ ft. high; stems upright and spikes close together; leaves narrow. In bogs.

3. *Carex collinsii* Nutt. 1¼ ft. high; slender, with few flowers in each spike; leaves very narrow. In bogs.

4. *Carex intumescens* Rudge. 2½ ft. high; stem upright or somewhat reclining, with mostly two round fertile spikes 1 in. in diameter; pouches strongly spreading, green. In wet pastures and swamps.

5. *Carex grayii* Carey. 2½ ft. high; dark green, stout; one or two spikes; leaves wider ¼ in. or more; otherwise like No. 4.

6. *Carex lupulina* Muhl. 3 ft. high; stout and leafy, upright or reclining; spikes two to four, oblong, 2 in. long, densely flowered, short-stalked. In wet grounds.

7. *Carex lupuliformis* Sartw. 2½ ft. high; spike 2½ in. long; differs from No. 6 in the seed, which is longer than wide in *lupulina*, and about as wide as long in *lupuliforis*. Both similar to fig. 8, but ears erect.

8. *Carex bullata* Schk. 1¾ ft. high; stems slender, sharp and rough-angled; spikes, mostly two, light green or straw colored, oblong, 1¼ in. long, ⅜ in. thick, shining; pouches spreading. In swamps.

9. *Carex tuckermanii* Dew. 3 ft. high; stems very slender; spikes two or three, 1½ in. long, ½ in. thick, oblong; otherwise like No. 8. In bogs and meadows.

10. *Carex retrorsa* Schw. 2 ft. high; stems roundish-angled and smooth; spikes three to five, 1½ in. long, ½ in. thick, oblong, three or four in a bunch at the top of the stem; otherwise like No. 8.

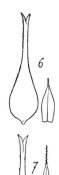

11. *Carex lurida* Wahl. 2¼ ft. high; stems roundish-angled, upright, slender; spikes yellowish green, one to four, oblong, 1½ in. long, ½ in. thick, densely many-flowered.

12. *Carex baileyi* Britt. 1½ ft. high; stem slender, upright or reclining; spikes one to three, long, oblong, densely flowered, 1½ in. long, ⅜ in. thick. In bogs.

13. *Carex hystricina* Muhl. 1½ ft. high; stem slender, sharp-angled; spikes one to four, long, oblong, 1½ in. long, ⅜ in. thick, somewhat nodding. In low meadows.

14. *Carex schweinitzii* Dew. 1¾ ft. long; yellowish green; spikes 2½ in. long, ⅜ in. thick, long, oblong, cylindric. In swamps.

15. *Carex trichocarpa* Muhl. 2½ ft. high; stem sharp-angled; spikes two to five, scattered, 2½ in. long, ½ in. thick.

16. *Carex lacustris* Willd. 3 ft. high; leaves broad and flat; spikes two to four, scattered, 3 in. long and ⅜ in. thick, varying to very short, the lower one drooping. In swales.

17. *Carex scabrata* Schw. 2 ft. high; leaves broad, flat and very rough; spikes three to five, 1½ in. long, ¼ in. thick, upright, the lower drooping. In moist woods.

18. *Carex pauciflora* Lightf. 1 ft. high; leaves very narrow, stems slender, upright; spike of only three or four downward pointed seed pouches below the upright sterile spike. In bogs.

Seed-pouch between ¼ in. to ⅛ in. long—
fertile spike globular, oblong.

19. *Carex oligosperma* Michx. 2 ft. high; stem very slender; leaves very narrow; one or two spikes, ¾ in. long. One sterile spike stalked, fertile spikes distant. In bogs.

20. *Carex hirta* L. 1¼ ft. high; stem slender, upright; two or three spikes, 1 in. long, ¼ in. thick, loose-flowered; lower leaves hairy; two or three sterile spikes stalked, fertile spikes distant. In fields and waste grounds.

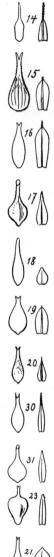

21. *Carex flava* L. 1½ ft. high; yellow-green; stem erect, very slender; one to four spikes, ⅜ in. long, ¼ in. thick; one sterile, sessile spike; fertile spikes close together. Swamps and wet meadows.

22. *Carex vestita* Willd. 2 ft. high; stems slender, erect or reclining; one to five fertile spikes, ¾ in. long, ⅜ in. thick; one sterile spike; seed pouch covered with hairs; spikes near together. In sandy woods.

Fertile spikes, oblong.

23. *Carex typhina* Michaux. 2½ ft. long; dark green; stems slender; leaves very broad; from two to five spikes, 1½ in. long, ½ in. thick, sterile flowers at the top and along the long stalk of the spikes. In swamps.

24. *Carex formosa* Dew. 1¾ ft. high; stem erect; the upper one sterile at its base; from three to five spikes; 1 in. long, ¼ in. thick, long-stalked, drooping, scale with short, rough awn. In dry woods.

25. *Carex castanea* Wahl. 2 ft. high; stem hair-like, somewhat reclining; one sterile spike, and from one to four fertile spikes, ¾ in. long and ¼ in. thick, long-stalked and drooping; leaves hairy. In dry woods.

26. *Carex languinosa* Michx. 2½ ft. long; stem slender, sharp-angled; from one to three spikes, 1 in. long and ¼ in. thick; pouch similar to No. 27, but wider. In swamps.

27. *Carex lasiocarpa* Ehrh., var. *americana* Fern. 2½ ft. long; stems very slender, reclining; from one to three spikes, 1 in. long and ¼ in. thick, far apart; seed pouch hairy. In wet meadows.

28. *Carex polymorpha* Muhl. 1½ ft. high; dark green; stems stiff and erect; from one to two spikes, 1¼ in. long, ⅜ in. thick, short-stalked. In swamps and meadows.

29. *Carex hirtifolia* Mackenzie. 1½ ft. long; bright green; stem slender, reclining; sterile spike, sessile; from two to four fertile spikes, ¾ in. long, ¼ in. thick, loose-flowered; leaves and pouch hairy. In woods.

30. *Carex rostrata* Stokes. 3 ft. high; stem stout, erect; from three to four spikes, 3 to 4 in. long, densely flowered, erect. In marshes.

66

PLATE XXVI

32

49

66.

8.

4.

31. *Carex vesicaria* L. 2½ ft. long; stem slender, reclining; from one to three spikes, 2½ in. long, ¼ in. thick, loosely flowered, spreading. In wet meadows.

32. *Carex comosa* Boott. 2½ ft. high; stem stout; from three to five spikes, 1¾ in. long and ½ in. thick, stalked, drooping, bristly, densely flowered; sterile spike, sometimes fertile at the top. In swamps and ponds.

33. *Carex davisii* Schw. & Torr. 2 ft. high; soft hairy; from three to four spikes, 1 in. long and ¼ in. thick, hair-like stalked, drooping; sterile spike, fertile at the top. In damp woods.

34. *Carex sprengelii* Dew. 2 ft. high; light green; from two to four spikes, 1¼ in. long and ¼ in. thick, loosely flowered, hair-like, long-stalked, drooping. On river banks.

35. *Carex arctata* Boott. 1¾ ft. long; stem slender, reclining; from two to four spikes, 1½ in. long and ⅛ in. thick, loose-flowered.

36. *Carex debilis* Michx., var. *rudgei* Bailey. 1½ ft. long; stem very slender, reclining; from two to four spikes, 2 in. long and ¼ in. thick, very loose-flowered, drooping; sterile spike, sometimes fertile at the top. In woods.

Seed pouch ⅛ in. long or less.—Spikes cylindrical.

37. *Carex acutiformis* Ehrh. 2½ ft. high; stem stout, sharp-angled, pale green; from one to three spikes, 2½ in. long and 3-16 in. thick, drooping or spreading; leaves broad and long. In wet meadows.

38. *Carex torta* Boott. 2¼ ft. high; stem slender, erect or reclining, light green; from three to five spikes, 2 in. long and ⅛ in. thick; beak of seed pouch twisted. In shady woods and marshes.

39. *Carex prasina* Wahl. 1¾ ft. high; stem slender, reclining, sharp, three-angled; from two to three spikes, 2 in. long and ⅛ in. thick; loose-flowered. In meadows and moist woods.

40. *Carex laxiflora* Lam. 1¼ ft. high; pale green, stem reclining; from two to four spikes, ¾ in. long and ⅛ in. thick; very loose and scattered and beset with flowers, drooping. In meadows.

68

Spikes oblong, globular.

41. *Carex oligocarpa* Schk. 14 in. high; stem hair-like, reclining, very slender; from two to four spikes, far apart, ½ in. long and ⅛ in. thick, upright; few-flowered. In dry woods and thickets.

42. *Carex viridula* Michx. 10 in. high; bright green; stems slender, upright; from two to four spikes, ¼ in. long and ⅛ in. thick. In bogs and damp rocks.

43. *Carex communis* L. H. Bailey. 1 ft. high; stems slender, reclining; from two to four spikes, very short, about ⅛ in. in diameter; pouch hairy. In dry grounds.

44. *Carex pensylvanica* Lam. 1 ft. high; dark green; slender, upright; sterile spike, ¾ in. long and stout; fertile spikes, one to three, small, ⅛ in. in diameter.

45. *Carex novae-angliae* Schw. 7 in. high; dark green, erect or reclining; sterile spike very narrow, fertile spikes two to four, small, globular, few flowered, with hairlike bracts double the length of spike. Damp woods.

46. *Carex umbellata* Schk. 2 in. high; leaves often 1 ft. long; grows in dense mats; stem with a bunch of several stemlets, each bearing from one to three very small spikes.

47. *Carex backii* Boott. 1 in. high; forming dense mats, stems sometimes hair-like and long; spikes of about three sterile and three fertile flowers, supported by a broad leaf-like bract. In woods.

Spike 1 inch or more long.

48. *Carex paleacea* Wahl. 1¼ ft. high; stem stout or slender, light green; from two to four spikes 2 in. long and ½ in. thick, often sterile at the top, drooping. In salt meadows.

49. *Carex crinita* Lam. 3½ ft. high; stem stout, 3-angled, erect or recurving; spikes three or five, 8 in. long and ⅜ in. thick, densely flowered, drooping. In wood swamps.

50. *Carex gynandra* Schw. 3 ft. high; stem stout; from three to five spikes 3 in. long and very narrow, drooping, resembling a *crinita*. In swamps.

69

51. *Carex tetanica* Schk. 1½ ft. high; light green; stem slender, erect; two or three spikes, 1 in. long, very slender, loose-flowered and drooping. In meadows.

52. *Carex stricta* Lam. 3 ft. high. In dense clumps; from two to four spikes 1½ in. long and ⅛ in. thick, narrow, cylindrical. In meadow swamps.

53. *Carex aquatilis* Wahl. 3 ft. high; pale green, stout, sharp, 3-angled; from two to four spikes, 2 in. long and ¼ in. thick, upright. In swamps along streams.

54. *Carex salina* Wahl. 2 ft. high; stem stout, erect; two to four spikes, 2 in. long and ¼ in. thick, upright. In marshes near the coast.

55. *Carex virescens* Muhl. 2 ft. long; stem slender, spreading; leaves hairy; two to four spikes, 1 in. long and ⅛ in. thick, narrow, cylindrical, spreading; sterile spike, fertile at the top. In woods.

56. *Carex gracillima* Schw. 2 ft. long; stem slender, spreading; three to five spikes, 2 in. long and ⅛ in. thick, narrow, cylindrical, drooping. In wet woods and meadows.

57. *Carex aestivalis* M. A. Curtis. 1½ ft. high; stem hairlike, slender; three to five spikes, 1½ in. long and ⅛ in. thick, spreading; end spike sterile at top and bottom. Mountain woods.

Fertile spikes ¼ in. or more thick, ½ to 1 in. long.

58. *Carex buxbaumii* Wahl. 2 ft. high; stem slender, 3-angled; two to four spikes, erect, sessile or very short stalked, ⅜ in. long, the upper spike sterile at the lower end. In bogs.

59. *Carex limosa* L. 1½ ft. high; stem slender, erect, light green; one or two hairlike-stalked drooping spikes, ¾ in. long and ¼ in. thick, one erect sterile spike. In bogs.

60. *Carex paupercula* Michaux. 1¼ ft. high; stem slender, reclining, one to three long-stalked drooping roundish spikes, ½ in. long and ¼ in. thick; one sterile spike. In bogs.

61. *Carex hirsutella* Mackenzie. 2 ft. high; light green, stem slender, reclining; two to five spikes ½ in.

long and ¼ in. thick, clustered at end of stem, the upper one sterile at the lower part.

Between ¼ and ⅛ of an inch thick.

62. *Carex haydenii* Dew. 1½ ft. high; stem slender, 3-angled; two to four spikes, ¾ in. long, sessile, cylindrical. In swamps and meadows.

63. *Carex nigra* (L.) Reich. 1½ ft. high; stem stiff, erect, sharp-angled; one sterile and two to three fertile spikes, sessile, narrow, cylindrical. In wet grounds.

64. *Carex amphibola* Stend. 1¾ ft. long; stem stout, erect, spreading, light green; one sterile and three to five fertile spikes, the upper ones close together, sessile, the lower long-stalked and distant, oblong. In woods.

65. *Carex flaccosperma* Dew., var. *glaucodea* (Tuck.) Kükenth. 1 ft. long; stem stout, spreading, pale, with bloom; one sterile and three to five fertile spikes, oblong, the lower stalked and distant, the upper sessile. In fields.

66. *Carex swanii* (Fern.) Mackenzie. 1 ft. high; stem very slender, erect or reclining; two to five spikes, oblong, ¾ in. long, the upper ones sterile on lower part, pouch hairy. In dry woods.

67. *Carex granularis* Muhl. 1½ ft. long; stem light green, slender, spreading; one sterile and three to five fertile spikes, the upper ones close, sessile, the lower ones distant, long-stalked.

68. *Carex crawei* Dew. 9 in. high; stems stiff; several sterile and one to four fertile spikes, upper sessile, the lower distant and long-stalked. Moist meadows.

69. *Carex pallescens* L. 1 ft. high, light green; stem slender, erect; one sterile and two to four fertile spikes, slender-stalked, oblong, clustered. In fields.

70. *Carex conoidea* Schk. 1 ft. high; stem slender, stiff, erect; one sterile and one to three fertile spikes, oblong, upper close, sessile, the lower distant, stalked. In meadows.

71. *Carex hitchcockiana* Dew. 1 ft. high; stems slender, erect; one sterile and two to three fertile spikes, very loose and scattering flowered, upper part of sheath swollen. In woods.

71

72. *Carex albursina* Sheld. 1½ ft. high; stem stout; leaves 1 in. or more wide; two to four spikes, very loose-flowered, upper sessile, lower short-stalked. In woods.

73. *Carex abscondita* Mackenzie. 4 in. high; stem very slender, erect; lower leaves ⅜ in. wide and longer than the stem; spikes very few-flowered, loose and slender.

74. *Carex panicea* L. 1½ ft. high, pale bluish green; one or two sterile and two to three fertile spikes, loosely many-flowered, oblong, cylindrical, the lower ones stalked. In fields.

75. *Carex livida* (Wahl.) Willd. 1½ ft. high, pale green; stem slender, erect; one sterile and one to three fertile spikes, two close together at end of stem, sessile, erect. In bogs.

⅛ of an inch thick or less.

76. *Carex digitalis* Willd. 1 ft. long; stem slender, thread-like; one sterile and two to three fertile spikes, slender-stalked and loosely flowered. In woods.

77. PLANTAINLEAVED SEDGE. *Carex plantaginea* Lam. 1 ft. long, dark green; leaves very broad; one sterile and three to four fertile spikes, loosely flowered, bracts with swollen purplish sheaths.

78. GOLDEN FRUITED SEDGE. *Carex aurea* Nutt. 8 in. long; stem reclining, slender; spikes few and loosely-flowered; seed pouch white when young, yellow when older. In wet meadows.

Spike less than ½ in. long.

79. *Carex laxiculmis* Schw. 1¼ in. long, blue green, with hair-like stems; lower leaves ½ in. wide; one sterile and two to four oblong globular fertile spikes, the upper one sessile, the other ones on very long hairlike stems, drooping. In woods.

80. *Carex eburnea* Boott. 10 in. long; stem thread-like, weak; leaves hair-like; one sterile and two to four fertile spikes ¼ in. long and less than ⅛ in. thick, stalked. In sandy soil.

81. *Carex pedunculata* Muhl. 6 in. long, in dense mats, bright green; stem very slender; one sterile and several few-flowered spreading drooping spikes ¼ in. long.

PLATE XXVII

82. *Carex deflexa* Hornem. 6 in. long; stem thread-like, bright green; one sterile and one to four fertile spikes ⅛ in. long. In mountains.

83. *Carex caryophyllea* Lat. 7½ in. long, dark green; stem very slender; one large sterile and one to three fertile spikes ⅜ in. long, all clustered at end of stem. Spikelet sterile at the top and fertile at the bottom.

84. *Carex willdenowii* Schk. 3 in. high, pale green; one to five spikes ½ in. long; leaves ⅛ in. wide and 1 ft. long. In dry woods.

85. *Carex leptalea* Wahl. 1 ft. high, light green; one spike ½ in. long; stem and leaves thread-like. In swamps.

86. *Carex exilis* Dew. 1½ ft. high; stem hair-like, slender, upright; one spike one inch long. In bogs near the coast.

87. *Carex chordorrhiza* L.f. 1 ft. long; roots creeping; stems upright; two to four spikes ⅜ in. long; leaves short. In bogs and shallow water.

88. *Carex stipata* Muhl. 2¼ ft. high; spike three inches long, with numerous many-flowered spikelets; beak ¼ in. long; seed-pouch rough, long and flat. In swamps.

89. *Carex diandra* Schr. 1¾ ft. long; spike 1½ in. long, with numerous oblong spikelets. In swamps and wet meadows.

90. *Carex vulpinoidea* Michx. 2 ft. long; stem sharply triangular; spike 3½ in. long, spikelets many, ⅜ in. long, oblong, each with a long, bristle-like bract. In swamps.

91. *Carex annectens* Bickn. 3 ft. high; spike 1½ in. long; stem stout; spikelets oblong egg-shaped. In fields.

92. *Carex setacea* Dew. 2¼ ft. high; spike 2 in. long; spikelets many, ¼ in. long, egg-shaped.

93. *Carex disperma* Dew. 1 ft. high; stem hair-like, rough; spikelets very small and far apart. In bogs.

94. *Carex rosea* Schk. 1½ ft. high, bright green; four to eight spikes, round, ¼ in. in diameter. In woods.

95. *Carex retroflexa* Muhl.   1 ft. high; four to eight spikes, round, ¼ in. in diameter; stem and leaves hair-like, short.   In thickets.

96. *Carex spicata* Huds.   1¾ ft. high; five to ten spikes, round, ¼ in. long; leaves narrow and long; stem upright or reclining.   Meadows and fields.

97. *Carex sparganoioides* Muhl.   5½ ft. high; stem rough, sharp, 3-angular, upright: leaves broad; six to twelve egg-shaped spikes.   In woods.

98. *Carex cephaloidea* Dew.   2½ ft. high; stem upright, slender; four to eight spikes, 1 in. long; bracts bristle-like, short; pouch 3-16 in. long.   Fields.

99. *Carex cephalophora* Muhl.   1½ ft. long; spikes many, close together, ½ in. long.   In dry fields.

100. *Carex muhlenbergii* Schk.   1¼ ft. high; stems light green, sharp, 3-angular, slender, upright; spike 1 in. long; bractlets longer than seed pouches, rough, bristle-like.   In dry fields.

Spikelets fertile at the top and sterile at the bottom.

101. *Carex cephalantha* (L. H. Bailey) Bickn.   1 ft. high; three to five spikes, round, far apart, ¼ in. in diameter.   In moist soil.

102. *Carex atlantica* L. H. Bailey.   1¾ ft. high; four to seven spikes, round, distant, ¼ in. long.   In swamps.

103. *Carex interior* L. H. Bailey.   1¾ ft. high; two to four spikes, round, distant, 3-16 in. long.   In wet soil.

104. *Carex canescens* L.   1¾ ft. high, pale green; four to nine spikes; ¼ in. in diameter, distant.   In swamps.

105. *Carex deweyana* Schw.   1½ ft. high; three to six spikes, oblong, ¼ in. long; last leaf as long as spike. In dry woods.

106. *Carex bromoides* Schk.   1½ ft. long; three to six spikes, ½ in. long, ⅛ in. thick; seed pouch ¼ in. long. In bogs.

107. *Carex siccata* Dew.   1½ ft. high; three to six spikes, ¼ in. long, short oblong.   In dry fields.

108. *Carex tribuloides*. Wahl.   1¾ ft. high; six to many spikes, ⅜ in. long and ¼ in. thick; pouch ¼ in. long. In meadows.

109. *Carex scoparia* Schk. 1½ ft. long; three to nine spikes, oblong, pointed at both ends, ½ in. long and ¼ in. thick; pouches ¼ in. long. In moist soil.

110. *Carex leporina* L. 1¼ ft. high; four to six spikes, ⅜ in. long and ¼ in. thick, close together; pouch 3-16 in. long.

111. *Carex cristatella* Britt. 2 ft. high; six to many spikes, round egg-shaped, ¼ in. thick; pouch 3-16 in. long. In meadows.

112. *Carex argyrantha* Tuckerm. 2¼ ft. high; four to many spikes, round egg-shaped, ¼ in. thick, far apart. In dry woods.

113. *Carex straminea* Willd. 1¾ ft. high; three to six spikes, ¼ in. thick, round egg-shaped, distant. In dry fields.

114. *Carex silicea* Olney. 1¾ ft. high; five to eight spikes, ½ in. long and ¼ in. thick, pointed at both ends; pouch 3-16 in. long.

115. *Carex tenera* Dew. 1½ ft. high; four to six spikes, round egg-shaped, ⅜ in. long, distant. In brackish marshes.

116. *Carex festucacea* Schk. 2½ ft. high; three to eight spikes, ¼ in. in diameter, close together. In dry or wet soil.

117. *Carex alata* Torr. 2¼ ft. high; spikes round egg-shaped, ½ in. long and ⅜ in. thick; seed pouch ¼ in. long. In moist grounds.

118. *Carex albolutescens* Schw. 1½ ft. high; three to eight spikes, short oblong, ⅜ in. long and ¼ in. thick, close; seed pouch 3-16 in. long. Wet soil.

NOTE.—Very similar to each other in the appearance of the ear are Nos. 1 to 3, 4 and 5, 6 to 12, 14 and 16, and 15, 17, 23, 30, 31, 52, 53, 62, 63. In Nos. 1 to 3, the spikes are loose, in 4 and 5 close and globular; in Nos. 6 to 12, 14 and 16 the spikes are dense, oblong and long-beaked, while in 15, 17, 23, 30, 31, 52, 53, 62 and 63 they are short-beaked. Nos. 13, 25, 32 to 39, 48 to 50, 54 to 57, 59 and 60 are drooping, and 18, 40, 41, 71 and 78 are few-flowered. Nos. 20 to 22, 24, 26, 28, 42, 51, 58, 61, 64 to 70, 74 and 75 have stout ears. Nos. 19, 29, 43 to 47, 72, 73, 76, 77, 79 to 86, 93 to 95 and 99 are like *C. pensylvanica*; Nos. 87 to 92 and 108 like *C. vulpina*, and Nos. 96 to 98, 100 to 107, 109 to 118 like *C. leporina*.

RUSH FAMILY. *Juncaceae.*

Plants with flowers from the side of the stem.

Flowers single on the branches of the bunch.

1. SOFT RUSH. *Juncus effusus* L. 2½ ft. high, stout, grows in tufts. In swamps and wet grounds everywhere.

2. THREAD RUSH. *Juncus filiformis* L. 1 ft. high; stems thread-like, roots creeping; flowers few, small and single on the simple branches of the bunch. In the mountains.

3. *Juncus arcticus* Willd. 1½ ft. high, with creeping roots. In size and appearance between Nos. 1 and 2. Near the shore.

Flowers in small clusters on the branches of the bunch.

4. *Juncus maritimus* Lam. 2½ ft. high, stout; branches of the flower bunch long and straight, and the bunch supported by long bracts. On the sea shore.

Plants with flowers on the top of the stem.

Flowers single on the branches, though often in clusters.

5. BROWNFRUITED RUSH. *Juncus pelocarpus* E. Meyer. 1 ft. high; stems thread-like. On the margins of ponds.

6. PATH RUSH. *Juncus tenuis* Willd. 1 ft. high; stems wiry. Everywhere in the wood roads.

7. TOAD RUSH. *Juncus bufonius* L. 7 in. high; flowering bunches one-third of the size of the plant; stems like No. 6, with short instead of long bracts. In dried-up ponds and damp roads.

8. HIGHLAND RUSH. *Juncus trifidus* L. 8 in. high; like No. 6, with only one or two flowers in the axis of bracts. In mountains.

9. *Juncus greenei* Oakes & Tuck. 1¼ ft. high; in dense tufts, with slender, round leaves which are channeled on the upper side; scales of the fruit pointed and shorter than the fruit-flowers, mostly sessile. Near the coast.

10. BLACK GRASS. *Juncus gerardii* Loisel. 1½ ft. high; like No. 9, but with creeping roots; flat leaves; mostly long-stemmed flowers. Scales shorter than fruit but rounded. Abundant in salt marshes.

11. FORKED RUSH. *Juncus dichotomus* Ell. 2 ft. high; like No. 9, but densely tufted, and flowers sessile, but larger; the scales as long as fruit and pointed; branches of bunch straight and long, and bracts short. Near the coast.

Flowers in close heads or bunches on the branches.

12. GRASSLEAVED RUSH. *Juncus marginatus* Rostk. 1½ ft. high; leaves flat; fruit capsule rounded at the top, and inner three scales

blunt and larger than outer scales, which are as long as, fruit and pointed; only few flowers in a bunch.   In grassy land.

13.   JOINTED RUSH.   *Juncus articulatus* L.   1½ ft. high; leaves round, pulpy, soft, with joints inside which can be felt, and on the lower part wilted leaves can be seen; many flowers in a bunch.   Near the coast.

14.   BAYONET RUSH.   *Juncus militaris* Bigel.   2 ft. high; like the last, but with hairlike leaves in the water, and round, jointed, stout leaves above.   In shallow ponds.

15.   ALPINE RUSH.   *Juncus alpinus* Vill.   1 ft. high; like No. 14, but scales shorter than the fruit and inner scales shorter than the outer.

16.   KNOTTED RUSH.   *Juncus nodosus* L.   1¼ ft. high; like No. 14, with only one or two heads; fruit larger than scales and inner scales larger than the outer.

17.   CANADA RUSH.   *Juncus canadensis* J. Gay.   2½ ft. high; leaves round and jointed, stem stout and hard, flowering late in autumn in dark red-brown heads, seed tailed on each end; scales one-third smaller than fruit.

18.   SHARP FRUITED RUSH.   *Juncus acuminatus* Michx.   2 ft. high; scales as long as fruit; seed pointed at each end.

PLATE XXVIII

INDEX OF GENUS
AND COMMON NAMES

A CATALOG OF SELECTED DOVER
BOOKS IN ALL FIELDS OF INTEREST

DRAWINGS OF REMBRANDT, edited by Seymour Slive. Updated Lippmann, Hofstede de Groot edition, with definitive scholarly apparatus. All portraits, biblical sketches, landscapes, nudes. Oriental figures, classical studies, together with selection of work by followers. 550 illustrations. Total of 630pp. 9⅛ × 12¼.
21485-0, 21486-9 Pa., Two-vol. set $25.00

GHOST AND HORROR STORIES OF AMBROSE BIERCE, Ambrose Bierce. 24 tales vividly imagined, strangely prophetic, and decades ahead of their time in technical skill: "The Damned Thing," "An Inhabitant of Carcosa," "The Eyes of the Panther," "Moxon's Master," and 20 more. 199pp. 5⅜ × 8½. 20767-6 Pa. $3.95

ETHICAL WRITINGS OF MAIMONIDES, Maimonides. Most significant ethical works of great medieval sage, newly translated for utmost precision, readability. Laws Concerning Character Traits, Eight Chapters, more. 192pp. 5⅜ × 8½.
24522-5 Pa. $4.50

THE EXPLORATION OF THE COLORADO RIVER AND ITS CANYONS, J. W. Powell. Full text of Powell's 1,000-mile expedition down the fabled Colorado in 1869. Superb account of terrain, geology, vegetation, Indians, famine, mutiny, treacherous rapids, mighty canyons, during exploration of last unknown part of continental U.S. 400pp. 5⅜ × 8½. 20094-9 Pa. $6.95

HISTORY OF PHILOSOPHY, Julián Marías. Clearest one-volume history on the market. Every major philosopher and dozens of others, to Existentialism and later. 505pp. 5⅜ × 8½. 21739-6 Pa. $8.50

ALL ABOUT LIGHTNING, Martin A. Uman. Highly readable non-technical survey of nature and causes of lightning, thunderstorms, ball lightning, St. Elmo's Fire, much more. Illustrated. 192pp. 5⅜ × 8½. 25237-X Pa. $5.95

SAILING ALONE AROUND THE WORLD, Captain Joshua Slocum. First man to sail around the world, alone, in small boat. One of great feats of seamanship told in delightful manner. 67 illustrations. 294pp. 5⅜ × 8½. 20326-3 Pa. $4.95

LETTERS AND NOTES ON THE MANNERS, CUSTOMS AND CONDITIONS OF THE NORTH AMERICAN INDIANS, George Catlin. Classic account of life among Plains Indians: ceremonies, hunt, warfare, etc. 312 plates. 572pp. of text. 6⅛ × 9¼. 22118-0, 22119-9 Pa. Two-vol. set $15.90

ALASKA: The Harriman Expedition, 1899, John Burroughs, John Muir, et al. Informative, engrossing accounts of two-month, 9,000-mile expedition. Native peoples, wildlife, forests, geography, salmon industry, glaciers, more. Profusely illustrated. 240 black-and-white line drawings. 124 black-and-white photographs. 3 maps. Index. 576pp. 5⅜ × 8½. 25109-8 Pa. $11.95

THE BOOK OF BEASTS: Being a Translation from a Latin Bestiary of the Twelfth Century, T. H. White. Wonderful catalog real and fanciful beasts: manticore, griffin, phoenix, amphivius, jaculus, many more. White's witty erudite commentary on scientific, historical aspects. Fascinating glimpse of medieval mind. Illustrated. 296pp. 5⅜ × 8¼. (Available in U.S. only) 24609-4 Pa. $5.95

FRANK LLOYD WRIGHT: ARCHITECTURE AND NATURE With 160 Illustrations, Donald Hoffmann. Profusely illustrated study of influence of nature—especially prairie—on Wright's designs for Fallingwater, Robie House, Guggenheim Museum, other masterpieces. 96pp. 9¼ × 10¾. 25098-9 Pa. $7.95

FRANK LLOYD WRIGHT'S FALLINGWATER, Donald Hoffmann. Wright's famous waterfall house: planning and construction of organic idea. History of site, owners, Wright's personal involvement. Photographs of various stages of building. Preface by Edgar Kaufmann, Jr. 100 illustrations. 112pp. 9¼ × 10.
23671-4 Pa. $7.95

YEARS WITH FRANK LLOYD WRIGHT: Apprentice to Genius, Edgar Tafel. Insightful memoir by a former apprentice presents a revealing portrait of Wright the man, the inspired teacher, the greatest American architect. 372 black-and-white illustrations. Preface. Index. vi + 228pp. 8¼ × 11. 24801-1 Pa. $9.95

THE STORY OF KING ARTHUR AND HIS KNIGHTS, Howard Pyle. Enchanting version of King Arthur fable has delighted generations with imaginative narratives of exciting adventures and unforgettable illustrations by the author. 41 illustrations. xviii + 313pp. 6⅛ × 9¼. 21445-1 Pa. $5.95

THE GODS OF THE EGYPTIANS, E. A. Wallis Budge. Thorough coverage of numerous gods of ancient Egypt by foremost Egyptologist. Information on evolution of cults, rites and gods; the cult of Osiris; the Book of the Dead and its rites; the sacred animals and birds; Heaven and Hell; and more. 956pp. 6⅛ × 9¼.
22055-9, 22056-7 Pa., Two-vol. set $21.90

A THEOLOGICO-POLITICAL TREATISE, Benedict Spinoza. Also contains unfinished *Political Treatise*. Great classic on religious liberty, theory of government on common consent. R. Elwes translation. Total of 421pp. 5⅜ × 8½.
20249-6 Pa. $6.95

INCIDENTS OF TRAVEL IN CENTRAL AMERICA, CHIAPAS, AND YUCATAN, John L. Stephens. Almost single-handed discovery of Maya culture; exploration of ruined cities, monuments, temples; customs of Indians. 115 drawings. 892pp. 5⅜ × 8½. 22404-X, 22405-8 Pa., Two-vol. set $15.90

LOS CAPRICHOS, Francisco Goya. 80 plates of wild, grotesque monsters and caricatures. Prado manuscript included. 183pp. 6⅝ × 9⅝. 22384-1 Pa. $4.95

AUTOBIOGRAPHY: The Story of My Experiments with Truth, Mohandas K. Gandhi. Not hagiography, but Gandhi in his own words. Boyhood, legal studies, purification, the growth of the Satyagraha (nonviolent protest) movement. Critical, inspiring work of the man who freed India. 480pp. 5⅜ × 8½. (Available in U.S. only)
24593-4 Pa. $6.95

SIR HARRY HOTSPUR OF HUMBLETHWAITE, Anthony Trollope. Incisive, unconventional psychological study of a conflict between a wealthy baronet, his idealistic daughter, and their scapegrace cousin. The 1870 novel in its first inexpensive edition in years. 250pp. 5⅜ × 8½. 24953-0 Pa. $5.95

LASERS AND HOLOGRAPHY, Winston E. Kock. Sound introduction to burgeoning field, expanded (1981) for second edition. Wave patterns, coherence, lasers, diffraction, zone plates, properties of holograms, recent advances. 84 illustrations. 160pp. 5⅜ × 8¼. (Except in United Kingdom) 24041-X Pa. $3.50

INTRODUCTION TO ARTIFICIAL INTELLIGENCE: SECOND, EN-LARGED EDITION, Philip C. Jackson, Jr. Comprehensive survey of artificial intelligence—the study of how machines (computers) can be made to act intelligently. Includes introductory and advanced material. Extensive notes updating the main text. 132 black-and-white illustrations. 512pp. 5⅜ × 8½. 24864-X Pa. $8.95

HISTORY OF INDIAN AND INDONESIAN ART, Ananda K. Coomaraswamy. Over 400 illustrations illuminate classic study of Indian art from earliest Harappa finds to early 20th century. Provides philosophical, religious and social insights. 304pp. 6⅜ × 9⅜. 25005-9 Pa. $8.95

THE GOLEM, Gustav Meyrink. Most famous supernatural novel in modern European literature, set in Ghetto of Old Prague around 1890. Compelling story of mystical experiences, strange transformations, profound terror. 13 black-and-white illustrations. 224pp. 5⅜ × 8½. (Available in U.S. only) 25025-3 Pa. $5.95

ARMADALE, Wilkie Collins. Third great mystery novel by the author of *The Woman in White* and *The Moonstone*. Original magazine version with 40 illustrations. 597pp. 5⅜ × 8½. 23429-0 Pa. $9.95

PICTORIAL ENCYCLOPEDIA OF HISTORIC ARCHITECTURAL PLANS, DETAILS AND ELEMENTS: With 1,880 Line Drawings of Arches, Domes, Doorways, Facades, Gables, Windows, etc., John Theodore Haneman. Sourcebook of inspiration for architects, designers, others. Bibliography. Captions. 141pp. 9 × 12. 24605-1 Pa. $6.95

BENCHLEY LOST AND FOUND, Robert Benchley. Finest humor from early 30's, about pet peeves, child psychologists, post office and others. Mostly unavailable elsewhere. 73 illustrations by Peter Arno and others. 183pp. 5⅜ × 8½. 22410-4 Pa. $3.95

ERTÉ GRAPHICS, Erté. Collection of striking color graphics: *Seasons, Alphabet, Numerals, Aces* and *Precious Stones*. 50 plates, including 4 on covers. 48pp. 9⅜ × 12¼. 23580-7 Pa. $6.95

THE JOURNAL OF HENRY D. THOREAU, edited by Bradford Torrey, F. H. Allen. Complete reprinting of 14 volumes, 1837–61, over two million words; the sourcebooks for *Walden*, etc. Definitive. All original sketches, plus 75 photographs. 1,804pp. 8½ × 12¼. 20312-3, 20313-1 Cloth., Two-vol. set $80.00

CASTLES: THEIR CONSTRUCTION AND HISTORY, Sidney Toy. Traces castle development from ancient roots. Nearly 200 photographs and drawings illustrate moats, keeps, baileys, many other features. Caernarvon, Dover Castles, Hadrian's Wall, Tower of London, dozens more. 256pp. 5⅜ × 8¼. 24898-4 Pa. $5.95

AMERICAN CLIPPER SHIPS: 1833–1858, Octavius T. Howe & Frederick C. Matthews. Fully-illustrated, encyclopedic review of 352 clipper ships from the period of America's greatest maritime supremacy. Introduction. 109 halftones. 5 black-and-white line illustrations. Index. Total of 928pp. 5⅜ × 8½.
25115-2, 25116-0 Pa., Two-vol. set $17.90

TOWARDS A NEW ARCHITECTURE, Le Corbusier. Pioneering manifesto by great architect, near legendary founder of "International School." Technical and aesthetic theories, views on industry, economics, relation of form to function, "mass-production spirit," much more. Profusely illustrated. Unabridged translation of 13th French edition. Introduction by Frederick Etchells. 320pp. 6⅛ × 9¼. (Available in U.S. only) 25023-7 Pa. $8.95

THE BOOK OF KELLS, edited by Blanche Cirker. Inexpensive collection of 32 full-color, full-page plates from the greatest illuminated manuscript of the Middle Ages, painstakingly reproduced from rare facsimile edition. Publisher's Note. Captions. 32pp. 9⅜ × 12¼. 24345-1 Pa. $4.95

BEST SCIENCE FICTION STORIES OF H. G. WELLS, H. G. Wells. Full novel *The Invisible Man*, plus 17 short stories: "The Crystal Egg," "Aepyornis Island," "The Strange Orchid," etc. 303pp. 5⅜ × 8½. (Available in U.S. only)
21531-8 Pa. $4.95

AMERICAN SAILING SHIPS: Their Plans and History, Charles G. Davis. Photos, construction details of schooners, frigates, clippers, other sailcraft of 18th to early 20th centuries—plus entertaining discourse on design, rigging, nautical lore, much more. 137 black-and-white illustrations. 240pp. 6⅛ × 9¼.
24658-2 Pa. $5.95

ENTERTAINING MATHEMATICAL PUZZLES, Martin Gardner. Selection of author's favorite conundrums involving arithmetic, money, speed, etc., with lively commentary. Complete solutions. 112pp. 5⅜ × 8½. 25211-6 Pa. $2.95

THE WILL TO BELIEVE, HUMAN IMMORTALITY, William James. Two books bound together. Effect of irrational on logical, and arguments for human immortality. 402pp. 5⅜ × 8½. 20291-7 Pa. $7.50

THE HAUNTED MONASTERY and THE CHINESE MAZE MURDERS, Robert Van Gulik. 2 full novels by Van Gulik continue adventures of Judge Dee and his companions. An evil Taoist monastery, seemingly supernatural events; overgrown topiary maze that hides strange crimes. Set in 7th-century China. 27 illustrations. 328pp. 5⅜ × 8½. 23502-5 Pa. $5.95

CELEBRATED CASES OF JUDGE DEE (DEE GOONG AN), translated by Robert Van Gulik. Authentic 18th-century Chinese detective novel; Dee and associates solve three interlocked cases. Led to Van Gulik's own stories with same characters. Extensive introduction. 9 illustrations. 237pp. 5⅜ × 8½.
23337-5 Pa. $4.95

Prices subject to change without notice.
Available at your book dealer or write for free catalog to Dept. GI, Dover Publications, Inc., 31 East 2nd St., Mineola, N.Y. 11501. Dover publishes more than 175 books each year on science, elementary and advanced mathematics, biology, music, art, literary history, social sciences and other areas.